Swelling with Pride

"Loving Benjamin" by Gail Marlene Schwartz was first published in *How to
Expect What You're Not Expecting: Stories of Pregnancy, Parenthood and Loss*,
edited by Lisa Martin-DeMoor and Jessica Hiemstra. Victoria: TouchWood
Editions, 2013.

Caitlin Press Inc./Dagger Editions
8100 Alderwood Road, Halfmoon Bay, BC V0N 1Y1
www.daggereditions.com
Text and cover design by Vici Johnstone. Cover artwork © Steve Gribben
Printed in Canada

Caitlin Press Inc. and Dagger Editions acknowledge financial support from
the Government of Canada and the Canada Council for the Arts, and the
Province of British Columbia through the British Columbia Arts Council and
the Book Publisher's Tax Credit.

Library and Archives Canada Cataloguing in Publication

Swelling with pride : queer conception and adoption stories / Sara
Graefe, editor.

ISBN 978-1-987915-84-6 (softcover)

1. Sexual minority parents. 2. Gay parents. 3. Same-sex parents.
4. Transgender parents. 5. Gay adoption. I. Graefe, Sara, editor

HQ75.27.S94 2018   306.874086'6   C2018-903400-9

Swelling with Pride

Queer Conception and Adoption Stories

Edited by Sara Graefe

Dagger Editions

Praise for *Swelling with Pride*

Swelling with Pride is an anthology filled with powerful truths and generous insight, as queer parent pioneers share the stories of the creation of their families. Including the most intimate details and the decisions that went into becoming parents, *Swelling with Pride* is also a useful guide for anyone considering parenting in a queer context. There is heartache in these pages, as children are yearned for, lost, mourned; as adoptions are disrupted and families separate—but there is also joy, as carefully planned and passionately desired dream children are welcomed home. Despite the odds against them, many writers approach their quest with refreshing humour. Readers will find themselves cheering these families on, astonished by their determination and inspired by the triumph of love over homophobia, technological barriers and infertility.

—Rachel Rose, author of
The Dog Lover Unit

Swelling with Pride gives voice to the new generation of lesbian, trans and gender non-conforming folks transforming parenthood. Whether they create their families through pregnancy, adoption or fostering, are single, partnered or creating ever new configurations of parenthood, this anthology's contributors offer their truths with courage, commitment and compassion. Infused with a uniquely queer perspective, *Swelling with Pride* will be reassuring to both prospective parents, those grappling with the nitty gritty of complications in donor choices, twin pregnancies, adoption or miscarriage, and even for those who've wished for parenthood, but found it heartbreakingly elusive. *Swelling with Pride* will be a valuable resource in the growing cannon of queer parenting literature, tangible comfort for readers during one of life's most difficult, yet joyous, journeys.

—Rachel Pepper, author of
The Ultimate Guide to Pregnancy for Lesbians

This collection is a valuable and illuminating addition to the literature about queer families, whose contributors are generous with their insight and experiences.

—Bruce Gillespie, editor of
A Family by Any Other Name

For Amanda and Aidan

CONTENTS

INTRODUCTION

Sara Graefe

The following baby game was circulating around Facebook a while back. Perhaps you caught it in your social media feed:

Ok Moms! What's your baby story?!

Age I got pregnant?

Age I gave birth?

Due date?

Day I gave birth?

Natural or C-section?

Weight?

Sex?

Name?

To my queer eye, what immediately leaps out from this playful survey — other than perhaps some privacy concerns — is its blatant hetero and cisnormativity. Where are the fields for known or unknown donor? Fresh or frozen sperm? DIY or fertility clinic? Gestating parent? Questions like "How many cycles?" or "Age when I started TTC?" What about questions for folks, queer or straight, who become parents through adoption? And don't get me started on the gendered language and assumptions.

9

There's no straightforward path to LGBTQ2 parenthood. Just as every queer person has their own coming-out story, every LGBTQ2 family has a unique conception or adoption story. For most of us, having sex at fertile times of the month just isn't going to cut it. Biological and societal barriers have forced us to be creative as we seek to bring children into our lives. By the time a positive line shows up on the pregnancy test or a child is proposed to us for adoption, we've already run a marathon.

Swelling with Pride is the book I wish had been out there when my wife, Amanda, and I had our first conversations about making a baby. This was back in the mid-2000s, and while a number of books were available on the experience of queer parenting *after* conception or adoption, there was little about how LGBTQ2 families are formed in the first place. Quite by chance, we'd stumbled upon a copy of Rachel Pepper's *The Ultimate Guide to Pregnancy for Lesbians: How to Stay Sane and Care for Yourself from Preconception Through Birth* (Cleis Press), the world's first-ever pregnancy book for queers, now a bona fide classic. It became our life raft and bible from those early talks, through the roller coaster of trying to conceive and then the ups and downs of the pregnancy itself, right up until the happy day our son burst into the world. While Pepper's book did an amazing job of walking us through the nitty-gritty each step of the way, Amanda and I still hungered for diverse, first-person stories from other queers who'd been through the process before us. Because social media was still in its infancy (we didn't even have Facebook accounts yet), we gleaned what information we could the old-school way: we compared notes on finding donors and the merits of fresh versus frozen sperm over homemade hummus at dyke potlucks and chatted with friends who'd already crossed that elusive gateway into LGBTQ2 parenthood.

For queer folk, trying to build a family through conception or adoption can be an isolating, fish-out-of-water experience, where one is alternately invisible or conspicuously Other. From our earliest visits to the fertility clinic, Amanda and I couldn't shake the sense of having entered an alternate universe, some kind of hetero hell. We had our first real taste of being out as queer parents when shopping for my first set of maternity clothes. Amanda, who's only a year and a half older than me, was helping scour the racks, desperately trying to locate something not overly frou-frou or girly — no small feat given the abundance of bows, frills and plunging necklines — when the clerk mistook her for my mother. We both froze, momentarily thrown, before I stammered, "You mean, my partner?"

In hindsight, this was a seminal moment, confirming that as expectant queers, we had indeed entered a whole other world: we were gate-crashers into the heteronormative zone of pregnancy, childbirth and parenthood. As my growing belly started outing me as a mom-to-be, strangers — from that maternity store clerk to random people in the street and, frustratingly, even some of our health care providers — scrambled to figure out where Amanda fit into the equation.

Flash forward to two weeks before my due date, when Amanda and I attended an inspiring, affirming panel on queer conception and adoption. The event was hosted by Pomegranate Community Midwives in Vancouver (where we'd been receiving excellent, queer-friendly prenatal care) as part of their new Twats and Tots LGBTQ2 parenting speaker series. After nine long months of my mostly being assumed straight and Amanda invisible, the session was a welcome breath of fresh air. It was pretty much our first opportunity to connect with fellow queers (outside our close circle of friends) who'd either been through, were currently going through, or were aspiring to the same thing as us, and to celebrate the unique, diverse ways we build our families.

If only we'd had access to this earlier in the pregnancy, or while we were trying to conceive, I thought, shifting under the weight of my bulbous belly as I leaned in, listening with rapt attention to the speakers' stories. *If only tales like these were documented in a book.* Little did I know at the time, but in that moment, *Swelling with Pride* — the collection you are now holding in your hands — was conceived.

This anthology of creative non-fiction celebrates LGBTQ2 families and the myriad of ways we embark upon our parenting journeys. Written by queer women, trans and genderqueer folk from across Canada and the US, these honest, heartfelt, unabashedly queer stories cover a gamut of issues and experiences, including the varied paths to LGBTQ2 conception — from DIY methods at home with the so-called "turkey baster" to pricey medical interventions at the fertility clinic — and the daunting tasks of choosing a sperm donor and gestating parent, among other challenges. This anthology also portrays journeys to LGBTQ2 parenthood that start or end with adoption and the countless hurdles that go along with it: from surviving the homestudy process and dealing with systemic homophobia to transitioning an adopted child into a new home. There are tales of non-binary pregnancy, inducing lactation in the non-gestating parent, a bi couple experimenting with polyamory in their search for a sperm donor, a three-mom blended family, parenting a second time with a new partner, and shooting a birth video as a learning tool for expectant queers in the days before YouTube and Vimeo. There are also stories of grief, all too often suffered in silence, such as coping with infertility, pregnancy loss, stillbirth, chromosomal abnormalities and adoption breakdown. There are the journeys of the early mavericks who formed families under the radar when fertility clinics were not open to singles and lesbians, as well as the Gen X and Millennial queers who've become parents during the current Gayby boom. Together, these twenty-five candid, moving, thought-provoking stories celebrate what it is to be queer and give voice to both the challenges and joys of building an LGBTQ2 family in a predominantly straight, cisgendered world.

Although *Swelling with Pride* was conceived early in my own parenting journey, it has had a very long gestation. As the book goes to press, our son, unbelievably, is about to turn eleven. He's now a full-blown tween, with adolescence just around the corner. As many parents lament, *Where does the time go?* On top of having my hands full the past decade — juggling my other writing with a demanding teaching job and co-parenting a young child — the time wasn't right to birth this collection. A few short months after our son was born, my mother-in-law was diagnosed with terminal cancer, making our baby's early years even more of a gruelling blur than we'd anticipated. After my mother-in-law's death, as I briefly touch on in my story "Best Laid Plans," Amanda and I tried many years for another child, ultimately walking away after a devastating diagnosis of secondary infertility. The last thing I wanted to do during those years of fruitless trying and the long, painful grieving process that followed was to work on a book celebrating, among other things, queer conception and birth. But I eventually came to a place where I realized it would be healing to follow through on my initial impulse to curate this collection — and indeed, it was. What a tremendous pleasure and privilege to work with such a diverse, talented group of LGBTQ2 writers — writers who entrusted me with their heartfelt, intensely personal and life-altering family experiences. It has been profoundly moving and affirming to midwife these intimate, emotional, brazenly queer stories.

So much has changed over the last decade. More queers than ever are choosing to become parents and are creating wonderfully diverse families. There's a wealth of information online about fertility, conception and adoption, just a keyboard click away. Prospective queer parents are finding each other and sharing information through social media groups and online chats. I've encountered would-be LGBTQ2 parents who, outwardly at least, approach the conception process much more casually and confidently than my queer peers and I did even ten years ago. When Dagger Editions at Caitlin Press came on board as publisher in 2016, my biggest concern was that this book was no longer relevant. My fears were quickly allayed when I went for a haircut, of all things: my long-time stylist, a Millennial queer, confided that she and her wife were actively trying to start a family. They had found an LGBTQ2-friendly fertility clinic and were in the midst of wrestling with decisions around choosing a donor, as well as whether to start with intrauterine insemination (IUI) or else to fast-track straight to in vitro fertilization (IVF). "I wish your book were ready now!" she lamented. "None of our friends understand what we're going through."

Around this same time, my local chapter of Vancouver's Rainbow Refugee Society was raising funds to assist lesbian asylum seekers from Russia, where LGBTQ2 people and their children are being persecuted under the Kremlin's new anti-gay legislation specifically targeting queer families. South of the border, Donald Trump was voted into the White House along with Vice-President Mike Pence, where they have been systematically attacking years of progress forged by LGBTQ2 Americans toward full equality. These are stark, timely reminders that, in most corners of the world, queer people do not live as freely as we are privileged to here in Canada, and that as LGBTQ2 families in North America, we can never take our hard-won rights for granted. More than ever, it is time to for us to share our stories, document our experiences and make ourselves visible, not only to celebrate our diverse families and inspire would-be queer parents, but also to fiercely fight and hold our ground.

You have picked up this book for any number of reasons, reasons that only you can know. Maybe you are part of an LGBTQ2 family and are thirsting to see your lives and experiences represented on the page. Maybe you are thinking of starting a family, or are actively trying to conceive or adopt. Maybe you're a queer ally — a friend, neighbour, extended family member, health care provider or just a curious onlooker. Maybe you are a queer grieving infertility, pregnancy loss, stillbirth or adoption breakdown and are looking for solace within your own community. I hope there is something in these pages that resonates with each and every one of you — and, most importantly, that this book inspires you to share and celebrate your own unique family stories, loudly and proudly.

Sara Graefe, Vancouver, May 2018

Our First Call to the Fertility Clinic Went Something like This

Corinne L. Mason

Me: "Hi! I'm calling to check the status of a referral. My name is Corinne Mason."

Them: "Nope. We don't have anything."

Me: "It should be there. We saw our doctor over six weeks ago."

Them: "Nope."

Me: "Can you check again? Our doctor's name is Dr. Habish."

Them: "I'll check the pile on our fax machine."

Me: "Great!"

* long wait *

Them: "Oh, we have to send it back to your doctor because we can't process the form."

Me: "Is there a problem?"

Them: "I can't read your husband's name."

Me: "I don't have a husband."

Them: "Your boyfriend."

Me: "I don't have a boyfriend."

Them: "Awww, that is really too bad."

Me: "I have a partner."

Them: "What is her name?"

Me: "Rune." I'm too shocked to speak to the receptionist about pronouns or gender.

Them: "Rune? Rune? What a funny name! Honestly, this writing is terrible."

Me: "That is my writing."

Them: "We're booking into next year. You'll get a letter in the mail."

hangs up phone

AND BABY MAKES HISTORY

Susan G. Cole

1985

To be honest, the idea of having a child had never crossed my mind. I was a radical lesbian feminist activist and writer — and a member of one of Toronto's first all-women rock bands — whose life project was to make social change, not babies. And I assumed that, as a lesbian, having a family was not in the cards.

My partner Leslie, on the other hand, had always wanted to be a parent, and her relatively late coming out at the age of thirty was doing nothing to deter her. She was trained in early childhood education and had a strong bond with children. As we were falling in love — you know, romantic dinners, days in bed — and still not cohabiting, she told me that she was intent on having a baby.

This was a bit of a shock to me, as I was still resisting that we even live together, let alone have a family. Fiercely protective of my independence — and spooked by having been left too many times — I'd had a fantasy about separate apartments in the same house or some such arrangement. At the most.

"That's fine," said Leslie. "If you want to co-parent you can put a crib at your place."

Actually, she also said something akin to: "It doesn't matter what you want; I'm having a kid regardless." If I wanted to make a life with her, I was going to have to adjust.

My claim to independence went out the window quickly. Within a week of our first date we were hanging out every weekend, and within half a year we had moved into a house together in Toronto's Kensington Market. Things were happening at what I thought was breakneck speed and what Leslie perceived as a snail's pace. It wasn't a few months before she said it was time to get on with the birth project.

When we asked our male friends for sperm donations, they dreamed up excuses that were everything from amusing to distressing. Our favourite one was from a man who said he feared he'd have too much responsibility, which we read as an underlying fear he wouldn't be able to give up control. I had asked my brother Peter for a specimen but he said no, presumably, I thought, because his wife at the time couldn't handle the idea.

Sperm banks were charging ten thousand dollars a pop — *really?* Think of all that expensive stuff wasted through masturbation. And they weren't doing business with single women, let alone lesbians. Finally, my brother, now separated and co-parenting my niece, agreed to give us the gift. He was moved by Leslie's passion for becoming a mother. Peter, a physician who was already incorporating alternative health methods into his practice and who had, as the medical officer of health for Peel Region, made violence against women a public health issue, was also a radical guy. He understood how his donation could be the most important political — and liberating — act he could undertake.

The first time we planned to inseminate, Peter was supposed to produce the sperm at his home in the country and take it to our house. He thought he'd be clever by keeping it warm with the cigarette lighter in his car — but by doing so, he literally fried the sperm. So, we changed strategies and decided he'd visit us and produce the sperm at our house. He'd bring my four-year-old niece, who thought the main purpose of the visit was so that Leslie and I could take her for a walk through the maze of fruit and vintage stores in storied Kensington. We did love that, for sure; but we were basically just leaving Peter alone so he could produce those precious bodily fluids.

We had already been in contact with a midwife I'd met through my women's health activism. Vicki van Wagner, a groundbreaking practitioner, was instrumental in getting midwifery recognized by the province as a legitimate health service. She'd already demonstrated for us what to do. In retrospect, it's shocking how simple the procedure was, once we had the sperm warm enough (and not fried). All we needed was a syringe. (Don't call them turkey-baster babies. That giant utensil simply will not work.)

Leslie had confessed to me earlier that she wanted a girl, which astonished me. I assumed she didn't care as long as there was a baby at the end of the process. That conversation was one of the first of many that made me realize how having children can test a relationship. I'm not talking about the sleep deprivation and divvying up the childcare, but rather about how parenting can turn into a crash course on what you didn't know about your partner. I didn't care what the gender of our child was, but Leslie did.

Nonetheless, I researched how to time the insemination to increase the chances of having a girl: we were to inseminate a few days before ovulation. Male sperm are faster and get to the egg too soon; female sperm swim more slowly and get there right on time — or maybe they don't. When Leslie didn't get pregnant during her first cycle, she agreed we'd inseminate a few days before ovulation and exactly during ovulation to increase our chances of conceiving something.

After three months, the average number of cycles it takes to conceive, Leslie was pregnant.

1986

As soon as Leslie began to show, we realized that being pregnant — and then having a child — would mean we'd be coming out all the time, often to strangers.

"Oh, you and your husband must be so happy."

"Well, I don't have a husband. My partner's a woman," Leslie would say, and would then cause apoplexy when she explained exactly how she'd gotten pregnant.

I hadn't spoken to my parents about our project at all until the insemination had been successful. I phoned my mother.

"Hi there, I have some news. Leslie's pregnant and Peter's the sperm donor."

Never one to be all that emotionally demonstrative but ever the practical one (and always loving), the first words out of her mouth were, "Get a job."

We were going through the pregnancy, ecstatic and proud, knowing that we were pioneers. We were familiar, but never friends with, just one lesbian couple who had a child that wasn't from a previous straight marriage. We liked to refer to ourselves as lesbians who had created a baby from scratch.

I began writing about it and at one of the first of Nightwood Theatre's famous Five-minute Feminist Cabarets, I performed a stand-up routine about our adventure of getting pregnant (Peter frying the sperm got a huge laugh). It was a big hit and I realized that, far from causing my writing career to stagnate, motherhood could prove to be a very rich area for my creativity.

Beware such hubris.

During the fifth month of her pregnancy, Leslie was preparing to have her first appointment with a new obstetrician. As she walked out the door, I noticed that her belly hadn't grown that much and said to her, "It's weird, but you don't look pregnant." That was a premonition.

Leslie was supposed to go to work after the appointment, so I was surprised when I heard our door open an hour after she'd left.

"Les?"

Silence.

I came to the top of the stairs and looked down at her at the bottom. She could barely get the words out. "She couldn't find the heartbeat."

"Well, that sometimes happens, doesn't it?"

"I know it, I've lost the baby."

We went together for an ultrasound and Leslie had an appointment immediately after with her doctor. The baby had died. I was nauseous and angry — it seemed so profoundly unfair. One thing about "lesbian babies:" they don't happen by accident and they are deeply wanted.

Leslie would have to keep the fetus until it spontaneously miscarried. If the baby didn't emerge in ten days, she'd need to have a dilation and curettage (D&C), something she desperately wanted to avoid. The wait was excruciating and weird for Leslie. Something was terribly wrong although she never felt sick, per se. The cramps eventually came and our midwife Vicki arrived at the house to assist with the "birth." She said she'd let me know when she needed me for help. While I waited, I cleaned out every cupboard in our kitchen — strange what we think of attending to when we don't know what to do with ourselves. When Vicki called me, the small sac emerged and she handed me the dead fetus, which I put into a yogurt container — I hadn't thought of what to do with it. I was surprised by my desire to look: a boy, with one leg. Who knows what else wasn't quite right; nature had done its job.

That moment profoundly transformed my perspective on abortion. It's not that it changed my opinion about a woman's right to choose, only that I never again made the claim that an unborn fetus was not a life. There was no denying that what had emerged from Leslie's womb had at one time been a living creature. Shortly after Leslie miscarried, I embarked on a series of college debates with Gwendolyn Landolt, a lawyer for the right wing women's organization REAL Women. When the topic turned to abortion, she took ten minutes to make the case that a fetus was a life and when she finished, I waited a few seconds and said, "You're absolutely right." This made her jaw drop. Then I continued, "and women have the right to make life and death decisions about our own body."

Leslie and I learned a lot about miscarriage: its high frequency, how seldom it's talked about, and, consequently, the extent to which the trauma is easily dismissed. Leslie was inconsolable. My mother, always someone, as I've said, who was uncomfortable with major emotional displays, impatiently wished Leslie would snap out of her grief.

At the time Leslie was working with the children of wife assault survivors at a women's shelter. Devastated and unable to focus properly, she asked her obstetrician for a letter so that she could be granted a leave. Leslie's doctor was outrageous and blithely asked, "What do you need that for, apart from the fact that it's summer and who wants to be working now?" She did eventually agree to produce the document.

I felt a certain degree of guilt, having gone so public with our situation, and I feared we were being punished because I exploited our situation for creative gain. We paid the price. Many people asked us how the pregnancy was going, and we had to talk to many people we didn't know about our painful situation. But it's also true that, having shared our story with something like three hundred strangers, we got a tremendous amount of support, beautiful cards and messages from people we barely knew. We became aware of how many women were invested in our pregnancy, both politically — here was a way to transform the nuclear family — and personally. We could feel it, and it reinforced our belief in the strength of our community.

Leslie turned her grief into the creation of a spectacular garden along the tiny patio in the back of our house, where we had buried the baby.

1987

To be honest, as the person who had to be convinced to embark on the birth project in the first place, I half hoped we might abandon it — it had been so fraught and painful — and was surprised at how quickly Leslie wanted to try again to get pregnant. Silly me — nothing was going to stop her.

My brother, ready and able, stepped in again and within three cycles, Leslie was pregnant. We were more circumspect this time about our good news and became tenser as the pregnancy went along. Having had a late miscarriage, we weren't ready to celebrate when Leslie went into her second trimester, but by the time Leslie was in her sixth month, we started to believe that we really were going to be mothers.

But we were the only ones we knew who were in that situation.

As we edged toward the birth, our awareness of how unusual our lesbian pregnancy was intensified. We were the only lesbians in our prenatal class (of course), and when I went to buy a car seat, mentioning that I was going to be a mother in a month, the salesperson plainly didn't believe me. At a certain point I stopped explaining things to everyone. But our main worry was, as the only lesbian couple we knew with children, that we would become alienated from our own community.

Close to the due date our doorbell rang. It was Leslie's parents, randomly arriving for a visit. A half hour later, the doorbell rang again. My parents were dropping in. Fifteen minutes after that, my brother and sister-in-law turned up. We had a spontaneous tea party and when they all left I said to Leslie, "Wow, coincidence or what."

Well, it was a coincidence, yes, but it was also true that something powerful was attracting our family to our expectant household. Leslie went into labour the next morning and called Vicki, who asked how the long the space was between contractions. At that point, it was as much as twenty minutes. Leslie and I had been lying on the couch, her head on one end, mine on the other, and having the sweetest experience. Contraction, sleep, contraction, sleep. We called our best friends and mine screeched with excitement. "Please don't bring that energy here," I laughed. They joined us for a walk on what was an unusually hot Victoria Day weekend. The lilacs had bloomed early, and we picked a spectacular bunch.

Later, in the evening, with Leslie upstairs in the bedroom, the contractions came closer together. Vicki said that Leslie should get down the stairs because she might have trouble if she waited any longer. By then Leslie was crying out — it was an unworldly, holy howl, actually — with the pain. I remember she eventually had to inch down the stairs on her backside, moaning deeply. It was late at night and the windows were wide open. God only knows what the neighbours thought was going on.

At the hospital (we dispensed with the idea of a home birth after the miscarriage) I brought Leslie her raspberry juice ice chips and watched as she went through her monumental process. My memories, I'm sorry to say, have faded. (I remember that the baby's arm was stuck over her head, but the doctor was reassuring.) I do vividly recall the moment Molly emerged. Leslie had started to crown and I thought, "Great, a few more hours and we're in business." I'd seen exactly one birth video in which the mom had crowned for a full two hours. Not Molly. She suddenly slid out — splurted out — arm straight out, fist forward. And in a moment of awesome articulateness, I cried out, "It's the baby!" and then cried real tears.

A girl — Molly. When the doctor put her in Leslie's arms, Leslie asked me, "Am I dreaming?"

"No," I smiled, "you're not."

2018

My short monologue became a full-length play called "A Fertile Imagination" (read it in *Lesbian Plays: Coming of Age in Canada*, edited by Rosalind Kerr and published by Playwrights Canada Press). I had big fun going back to it recently and reading the story about two lesbian lovers, hard-assed feminist writer Del and the way more user-friendly childcare worker Rita, who are trying to have a baby. It was hit for Canada's women-centred theatre Nightwood for a number of reasons. Many of its themes resonated with audiences no matter their sexual orientation or gender. Soon-to-be fathers could relate to Del's growing panic over her partner's obsession with her pregnancy, sparking fears that after the baby was born, she'd lose Rita forever. Others connected to the duo's discovery, especially after Rita suggests that she wants a girl and might bring a Barbie doll into the household, that they may not share the same values about everything.

But it's the central theme that got to me: the couple's distress that they will be alone as parents in their community. Fledgling Dykes With Tykes groups don't appeal to them — they don't want new friends. As the play unfolds, they feel increasingly alienated, especially Del.

The play makes myriad pop-culture references which I thought I'd have to update whenever it was produced (seven different companies eventually staged it). But I see now that that's not necessary: "A Fertile Imagination" is now a bona fide period piece and should be staged with its original text, complete with references to Madonna's controversial Pepsi commercial.

There are now six million children with LGBTQ parents in the United States. Playgrounds at Pride celebrations all over our own country are swarming with children. It is now possible for two women to put their names on their child's birth certificate (for that matter, more than two parents can be registered) and, of course, gay marriage is now legal, a fact that very well may have paved the way for the waves of queer births.

And, for the record, our friends were loving and hugely helpful. It's true that when Molly was in her infancy, some of them cancelled babysitting appointments in cavalier ways that suggested they didn't get what was at stake when exhausted new moms Leslie and I couldn't get those precious few hours together. But those disappointments were extremely rare — and our beloveds have maintained close connections to our daughter.

My brother, a loving uncle who never intruded, died three years ago. Molly did know that he was her sperm donor. We told her when she was seven years old. We had been reading Lesléa Newman's *Heather Has Two Mommies* to her and every time we came to the part where the lesbian couple go to the doctor to get sperm, we considered telling her where she came from. Finally we asked her, "Have you ever wondered how we made you?"

"No," she replied, "you went to the doctor and got sperm."

Ah, the power of the story!

"No, your uncle Peter gave us the sperm."

Molly looked at us in wonder: "Someone I know!"

Molly is now married and extremely successful in her public relations career. She and Jon come to our house for dinner every week — and they're not happy when we have to cancel.

We pick lilacs every year before Molly's birthday.

THE MANY POSSIBLE VERSIONS OF YOU

Josephine Boxwell

Cells dividing and creating something greater until it gets so large it no longer fits and it has to come out. And it screams when it arrives because it had seemed so big before, but it is suddenly very small in the vastness of everything.

"She is gaye," the doctor writes. "Has female girlfriend. Needs sperm to bond baby."

My referral, obtained from a walk-in clinic in Prince George, BC. He crosses out "female," realizing the redundancy. We aren't from here and neither is the doctor. Being new to town, I haven't yet registered with a GP, but it is at this precise moment that I decide I should. The walk-in doctor, as polite as he is, doesn't understand the Ontario medical forms I present him with, even with the help of a receptionist he has summoned for her English fluency, and my situation, he explains apologetically, isn't one he has come across before. He trades in sniffles and sore throats, not sperm.

We could have adopted you. We could have brought you home aged two or five or twelve. We could have become part of the "flower model," as someone explained it to us, with you in the middle and the rest of us (biological family, foster parents and adopted parents) all circling you like petals. It isn't a broken system after all, but a garden bursting with flowers waiting to bloom. It sounds wonderful, and you would have been, if you came to us that way, but we were anxious about the years of assessments and evaluations that come before the flower arranging bit (not to mention the other petals).

We could have chosen a known donor. We asked someone, a close friend of mine. He grew up in a centuries-old thatched cottage in southern England. His parents still live there, and they have absorbed the low ceilings and dark little rooms into their minds like beetles burrowing into old wood. They couldn't begin to fathom the idea of our family made possible with the help of their son. They couldn't reach a place of acceptance — not only of you, but of him — if he chose to become a donor. In helping to create you, he would risk losing the closest members of his own family. They successfully quashed that possibility of you.

As we settle into this unfamiliar city, we choose "unknown donor" as our route to parenthood, and we sign up to a home insemination program provided by a Toronto-based sperm bank. We decide which one of us should try to become pregnant. Mommy could have carried you, but my biological clock has more time on it, and her maternal instincts are so strong she'll be carrying both of us anyway.

My Ontario referral form gets absorbed into the vast database of British Columbian medical documents, and I proceed to the next stage: tests. My blood gets lost between Prince George and Vancouver and Toronto, but eventually the sperm bank has what they need to cross their t's — clean results and credit card cash. They talk us into the bulk buy, six vials at a reduced rate, two per cycle.

We scroll through hundreds of profiles looking for the perfect donor, each one representing so many unique characteristics that could become part of your genetic other half. We examine personal essays, medical histories, personality test results and audio interviews. The voices of strangers follow us to sleep and echo through endless back-and-forth deliberations.

Specific traits do not, of course, come guaranteed, but would you be happier with looks or intelligence? Is height significant, or bone structure, and does "big boned" really just mean fat? What if larger people are actually happier? We wouldn't want you to be skinny and sad. One donor has supplied rather distracting baby photos of himself in which he resembles a small gremlin. I don't think we have ever been so judgmental of strangers, yet all of these individuals are doing something we could never adequately thank them for. They are helping families like ours bring little yous into the world.

We examine collections of jigsaw puzzle pictures: an eye in one photo, lips in another, then a torso. The puzzles are designed to protect the donors' identities. Which pieces are more dominant, genetically? My eye colour or this guy's? My nose or his? This donor has a nice nose, but what about the noses we don't see? What if buried somewhere in his ancestry there is an unflatteringly bulbous snout determined to make a comeback?

The US banks don't bother with puzzle pieces; we can see the donors' faces as soon as we sign in. We only get a complete view of our short-listed Canadian candidates when the consultant runs a Skype screen share with us. We have no choice but to put our trust in this doctor and his clinic, and the donors themselves, hoping that all the information we are given is reliable. Industry regulations on both sides of the border could certainly be improved upon.

Some donors are easily eliminated. Concerning medical disclosures (schizophrenia, childhood diseases) and bizarre causes of death in the family (gunshot wounds, asphyxiation) catch our attention, because while every clan has its struggles, there appear to be more serious issues lurking in those backstories. At least those guys are honest. We also eliminate individuals who disclose nothing, because that is impossible to believe. Then there are those with backgrounds or personalities we can't connect to, and those that are unwilling to meet you, if you want to, when you turn eighteen.

The audio interviews all follow the same pattern. The clinician trots out identical questions each time as though it might break his carefully constructed experiment if he were to alter his tone slightly.

"Who do you most admire?" he asks at some point in the middle. It doesn't take one donor long to decide, the twenty-four-year-old with a passion for real estate and no time for hobbies. He has prepared for this.

"Margaret Thatcher."

A young Canadian male who *most* admires, of all the people living and dead he could think of (and I can tell from his reasoned response that he has actually thought about it), Margaret Thatcher. I read an article once that claimed conservatism is genetic. I don't know if that's true, but why risk it?

The donor we choose is, according to the accumulated bits of his life presented by the sperm bank, smart, humble and averagely good looking. There's a chance you will have his blue-grey eyes or his aptitude for math or his love of reading. There's a chance you'll inherit his undisclosed short-sightedness or his great-great-grandfather's enormous nose.

The delivery guy pulls up in his knackered Ford Focus and drags a long box sideways out of the back seat. He drops the battered package on the doorstep. It's not exactly what I expected, but I sign for it, well aware that we're on the hook for another couple of grand if the tank inside is damaged when we return it. It's just another gamble. This is a process void of any guarantees.

We pull the tank out of the flimsy cardboard case. Inside is a cloud of liquid nitrogen and a chamber holding two tiny vials, each containing millions of genetic possibilities. Even after we've come so far, there are still many ways that you could become precisely you. The possibility also remains of you not becoming. We could run out of money before you even begin to form, and we will be trapped inside our hopelessness like addicts, obsessing over ways we could give it just one more try. I hope that if this path leads us nowhere, we can still be appreciative of technological advances, the laws of this country and the anonymous man who gave us this chance.

In a blink, we're down to our last two vials. The possibility of you existing is shrinking. It's a process, defrosting sperm. Did we correctly acclimatize it and inseminate and lay back and wait, hips slightly raised? Is it me? Am I preventing you from being? I could be biologically ill-equipped for this. Stress makes it harder to conceive. It is difficult not to get stressed when focusing on not getting stressed.

Our gormless stork returns with the last of our bulk buy. He approaches the house with the same worn-out cardboard box that we tape the hell out of each time before we send it back. As he dumps it on the doorstep, he hesitates. He motions his head towards the box.

"Mind if I ask what's in that?"

"Sperm," my partner tells him matter-of-factly.

A pause. Then, "Oh."

A moment later he folds his lanky body into the driver's seat of his understated delivery car. It is impossible to determine whether he is shocked, confused, amused or unimpressed, but it doesn't seem particularly surprising that the multi-national courier he represents hasn't yet entrusted him with a logo-emblazoned van.

I mistake pregnancy symptoms for pre-menstrual symptoms and am convinced you aren't there, but you are. A pee stick confirms it a couple of weeks later. We can't believe it. Half of you was previously frozen, like supermarket fish, and yet, here you are. You exist.

It isn't real. I can't feel you and I worry I could lose you by doing something wrong. Miscarriages are common early on, I read, and it isn't anybody's fault. You could just slip away, but you don't. You stay, and you grow. In the dating ultrasound, you aren't much bigger than a bean. We see you wriggle. We think about who you might be and how we will be with you.

I grow increasingly concerned about how my choices could be shaping your tiny self. You are still only partway to becoming. Avoiding alcohol is easy; it's the rest of it that opens up in front of me like a minefield. No sushi, limited caffeine intake, honey should be pasteurized. Herbal tea is a lot more complicated than I expected it to be. What about exercise? Lifting things? Shovelling snow? Online advice for expectant mothers is both abundant and contradictory, and now I'm attracting clickbait posts like "Why You

Should Never [Insert Something Everybody Does] With Your Baby." I lose the will to Google, and I can only hope you don't suffer any developmental consequences as a result.

The doctor can't find your heartbeat. She tells us not to worry, but we do, and she sends us to the hospital for another ultrasound. The technician explains coldly before she begins that she can't discuss the results with us — we will have to wait for our doctor to contact us, and she tilts the screen away so we can't see what she sees. It sinks in at that moment, that for some families, this is where it ends. Your little life is so fragile.

"It's fine," the technician announces suddenly. "There's a heartbeat." She swings the monitor around and asks if we want to know the gender.

You can hear us now and you are developing tiny brain cells. I should be talking to you more, and singing. Babies like songs. You get big enough to ripple my shirt as you squirm beneath my skin and we, your parents, begin to see ourselves differently. We will be Mommy and Mama and we will have a son.

We pick a room and paint it pale yellow and stick removable plastic forest animals on the walls. We fill it with things we think you might need and start calling it a nursery. I get big and uncomfortable and my hips ache when I try to sleep. We become inundated with labour horror stories; the boy who starfished his way to an emergency C-section, the five-day marathon, the girl who broke one of Mommy's ribs on her way out. We attend prenatal classes, except for the class for dads. We skip that one. Mommy doesn't want to spend two hours discussing her masculinity.

We wait for you to come, and as we count the days impatiently, "expectant mother" becomes an apt title for both of us. Mommy's hoping my British genes are so strong you'll pop out with an accent. I've told her that's unlikely, but you might end up with my frizzy hair, which for some reason she has also requested. Whoever you are, we'll be in awe, big nose or small, even if you develop an inexplicable fondness for Margaret Thatcher.

WHY I DIDN'T RUN AWAY
WITH THE CIRCUS

Vici Johnstone

When I was twenty-three, I dropped out of university to run away with the circus. At least, that's what I like to tell people. It is not entirely true, but neither is it a complete fabrication. I did run away, but not quite to follow the circus.

I grew up in Vancouver. I had four siblings and we all attended Killarney Senior Secondary School, one of the roughest schools in the city. Being queer and out was just not an option in the seventies, and definitely not an option in the east end of Vancouver. After graduation, I floated around Vancouver for a while, eventually finding the queer community — the underground bars with black doors, barred windows, disco music and, yes, polyester flare pants — and I had a few affairs. By the time I was twenty-three, I had been out for six years. But in doing so, I also made the decision to disappear from my previous life. I abandoned my childhood friends and distanced myself from my family. I had accepted that being queer meant three things: one, that I would likely be single most of my life; two, that invisibility offered freedom and safety; and three, that marriage and children were now off the table.

When the opportunity presented itself for me to join the cast and crew of John MacLachlan Gray's *Rock and Roll* on a tour across Canada, I knew I had found the perfect job: one that allowed me to keep busy and keep moving. I became a gypsy of sorts, always on the move, always stimulated by work and surrounded by other people who rejected traditional societal roles. The theatre community became my new family.

But in the late eighties, things began to change. The Pride movement was gaining momentum, parades celebrating our queerness were happening all over the country (though in Calgary, where I was now based, we still needed a police escort), and I had landed a job at Theatre Calgary as a permanent employee. Life was still a party — we worked hard and played hard — but some sense of stability had returned to my life. I was content, but deep inside, I longed for the comfort and confidence that comes from family life — like the family I had grown up with.

In my second year at Theatre Calgary, I began to date a woman who was the theatre's house manager and also a student at the University of Calgary. We had only been together a few months when she invited me to join a field study she was organizing to the Balkan countries. In a span of ten weeks, we were to visit what was then Yugoslavia, Bulgaria, Turkey and Greece. The wandering minstrel in me jumped at the opportunity.

As promised, our group of fifty students, led by a few rather renegade professors, travelled to some amazing destinations: Sofia, the Black Sea, Thessaloniki, Athens, Rhodes, Istanbul … Ironically, at thirty, my partner and I were among the oldest in the group, and not the only queers. There were two young queer men in our group as well and we became quick friends, together seeking out the unique destinations and quaint pensions off the beaten track. Todd and Mark were not lovers. Todd had a partner at home whom he spoke about often. He even carried a picture and made promises that when we were back in Canada we would all meet, and that we too would fall in love with Fraser.

True to his word, when we returned home at the end of the summer, Todd arranged a dinner party to introduce us to Fraser. He was right; Fraser was, and still is, a unique and lovable man. It was nice to have a queer couple as friends. We had many dinners together and shared stories about our life goals and our families.

My partner and I had talked about children. We had been hearing that lesbian women in Canada were finding ways. While it was not illegal in Canada for queer women to be inseminated, getting pregnant through a fertility clinic was not an option for anyone other than straight married couples. Ironically, it was not illegal to have sperm shipped across the border by Federal Express. We considered this option, but to me it felt too impersonal. I did understand why couples would want the anonymity, but I felt that I wanted a connection with the father. My partner was not so sure. But it all seemed a bit theoretical until Fraser told us that he would love to be a dad and, if we were interested, he was willing to help us get pregnant.

We initially thought my partner would be the birth mother (for the first baby), but then she developed some health conditions that the doctors felt might present complications. Suddenly, being a parent became a real and somewhat scary possibility. After many discussions, my partner and I decided that Fraser would be an amazing donor and I would be the birth mother. My partner was still uncomfortable about a father figure in our child's life. She was afraid that it would undermine her role as "the other mother." We found a solution when another queer friend also offered to "contribute to the cause." The solution of multiple donors, we decided, would offer the anonymity she needed, and at the same time the connection to the biological father(s) that I desired. The pieces were in place; now we just needed to sort out the logistics.

I don't really remember how we found Penny and Sue, and I have long forgotten their last names, but these two women were pioneers and advocates in the field of lesbian mothers' rights. Penny and Sue were single-handedly running the local chapter of the Lesbian Mothers Defense Fund (LMDF), an organization originally founded to help lesbians fight the law that challenged their custody rights when they divorced or separated from their previous male partners. Across the country, women who had been emboldened to come out of the closet by Pierre Trudeau's 1967 declaration "There's no place for the state in the bedrooms of the nation" were subsequently stripped of all rights to raise their naturally born children. The state, it seemed, was willing to stay out of the bedroom but also felt it had a moral right to protect children from their hedonistic mothers. By the time we met Penny and Sue, the laws had changed and while lesbian women were still (and are to this day) fighting custody battles over their children, the need for a nationwide legal fund had somewhat subsided. Sue and Penny turned their commitment, and that of the local LMDF, to helping queer women get pregnant.

Penny and Sue had a young son themselves and were a wealth of information. They had developed a wide range of resources for queers who wanted to become mothers and hosted a monthly information-sharing circle. They also managed some more practical services, such as running sperm in a double-blind scenario, so that anonymity could be completely maintained. They wrote and distributed pamphlets about fertility and when and how to inseminate (FYI, turkey basters were not recommended!), and they were available twenty-four hours a day for women who just needed to talk. My partner and I volunteered with the LMDF with a number of other lesbian couples, and eventually we collectively changed the organization to the Lesbian Mothers Support Society. Our goal was to create a community of support, not just for ourselves as we tried to get pregnant, but also for our children as they grew up. We were not so naive to believe that society would welcome our children and our non-traditional families with open arms.

With Penny and Sue's help, we developed a plan that would see the boys alternating donation nights. We carefully tracked my cycle, so we would know when I was at optimum fertility. When the time came, our plan worked like clockwork: sometime in the late evening, one of the guys would show up with a little jar carefully wrapped up in a wool sock. We inseminated five times over five days, and two weeks later, I started having morning sickness. Unbelievably, I got pregnant on our first try.

The pregnancy went as pregnancies go: I swelled up like a balloon and developed cravings for curry and apricots, both of which I had previously hated. My partner and I joined a Lamaze class, which definitely made some of the other participants uncomfortable, but the nurses were amazingly supportive.

In September of 1990, I gave birth to a beautiful blond-haired, blue-eyed baby boy, who is now almost thirty. We named him Dannen. Shortly after his birth, my partner and I were interviewed on what was then CBC Radio's *This Morning*. Our interview was part of a special program on alternative families. The day after the interview ran, my neighbour knocked on my door to tell me her mom, in Newfoundland, had heard our story and that it had changed how she viewed not only queerness, but also queer parenting. She said it had never occurred to her that we also desired family.

Fraser and his new partner, Doug, have been a constant and positive influence in Dannen's life. We have lost touch with the other donor, who made it clear from the beginning that he had no need to serve a role and felt confident the child was in good hands. My partner who was there with me in my biggest moment is no longer in my life. We split up and I gained sole custody of our son. It was a bitter legal battle, one that left me torn between upholding the rights of the queer community and my commitment to my son's well-being. I have not heard from her for many years, though she does occasionally contact Dannen.

In all honesty, I have to admit our son did have some struggles. He faced discrimination and confusion at times because he has both a mother and father who are queer. But he held his ground and as he grew, so did Canada's understanding of queer culture. Our son, and the children of the women we worked with in the eighties and nineties, live in a different world than when they were born. Queer parenting in Canada is widely accepted because of women like Penny and Sue who paved the way for queer parents like me and thousands of others. Our world has indeed changed. Our children are no longer so unusual, and being queer in Canada is no longer a definitive "well of loneliness."

Many years have passed since my theatre life. I have settled down a bit. I bought a house and a business, and my son has graduated from university. I still have this intense drive to keep moving — to see new things, meet new people. Fortunately, my work feeds this part of me. Fraser and Doug are also big travellers, so between his mother and father, our son has been lucky to see many amazing places in the world. As a graduation present, he asked for contributions to his travel fund, so it seems he has inherited the wanderlust from both sides of the family. It has taken me many years to realize that leaving something familiar does not have to mean you are running away. Sometimes leaving simply means you are reaching out for a bigger community.

Circumstances Beyond Our Control

Janet Madsen

Fertility Reach

"If you're waiting for the perfect time to have a baby, there isn't one," a friend with two kids offered, after hearing my latest instalment of the baby-when-and-how discussion series my partner and I had been having for months. I was ready to move forward; my partner less so. They argued that it's an enormous job and they wanted to consider all angles to make sure they were up for it. I knew they were right, but I was driven. The discussion series continued until we both had reached a point of feeling ready enough, which evolved over a year before we took the next step.

Being a queer couple wanting to reproduce means opening up your coupledom. Because you need a missing ingredient — in our case, sperm — you have to accept other players in what is usually an intimate process. I know there are heterosexual couples who deal with this disruption in the process too, because as much as we'd like to joke, fertility clinics weren't created exclusively for queers. The "plus one" might be a friend who becomes your donor, or maybe it's going to be a description and a number at the fertility clinic.

We found it interesting how needing outside help prompted some people to think they should have a say in how things would go. One person we knew felt we should use a friend of hers as a donor. We didn't know the guy and had no interest in the arrangement, but our friend couldn't see why not and was supremely pissed. She thought he was perfect.

We decided on a willing-to-be-known donor, something un-available in Canada at the time. A willing-to-be-known donor agreed to have identifying information available to his offspring when they come of age, should they want it. It sounded like the best option. We chose a donor and bought a six-pack of vials from a clinic in California that said they could ship it no problem.

That turned out to be impossible. Health Canada had changed the rules on sperm testing procedures just days before we made our purchase, unbeknownst to us or the clinic in California, and certainly wasn't going to bend the rules for us. They didn't care if the sperm was the same, and admissible, the week before (or that our purchase was explicitly non-refundable).

The California clinic explained that they tested the samples for the same STIs as Health Canada, but Health Canada changed their criteria for acceptable methods of testing. The clinic tried to argue our case for a couple of months, submitting all their testing procedures for scrutiny. We called Health Canada for progress reports to see if they would make the exception, but the answer to all of us was no. There was nothing we could do. The clinic recognized they were stuck and we were stuck, and they refunded our money. We were back to square one sperm-wise, but this time more determined.

We weren't happy, but accepted we'd have to go the anony-mous-donor route. We went to a fertility clinic that was reputedly queer-friendly and, in our experience, it was. We went through the intake process, which included a requisite session with a psychologist who acknowledged ours wasn't the usual tear-filled ones she'd previously had. We were given a book of possible donors and spent hours talking over attached and detached ear lobes, eye colours and personal essays. We chose our guy and happily anticipated starting insemination.

But alas, we were directed to wait.

Before I could start inseminations, I was required to have an HSG (the abbreviation of an incredibly long name for an x-ray of the fallopian tubes which hurts like hell). Once my doubled-over shaking and nausea subsided, we went to the clinic for the reading of the test. The doctor informed me that it looked like one of my fallopian tubes was blocked, so before the clinic would be willing to perform inseminations, they wanted me to have surgery to un-block the tube. My mother had borne four children in her forties, three of whom survived, so I wasn't worried about fertility until I was told to worry about fertility. Surgery? I still felt sick from the x-ray and was devastated to get this news.

Along the way we had found a queer moms' Listserv that included women from all over the world who talked all things pregnancy and child-rearing (it was also on this Listserv that my partner and I were introduced to Harry Potter. We read the first one aloud to each other while I was pregnant; we were hooked).

I loved those folks. They were funny, generous, open with their experiences of trying/getting/staying pregnant and also about mis-carriages and births. Those who already had children were similarly wonderful and we made many friends, many of whom we're still connected to eighteen years later.

We also met local queer parents and started up a group that had monthly potlucks and outings so kids could be around other queer families, as there weren't as many of us then. I love that many of those parents have known my kids since they were only thoughts. They have as much an investment (and humour) in their raising as we do.

After the HSG, I checked in with all the queer moms I knew and got all kinds of feedback on HSG results. Tubes could cramp and maybe it wasn't blocked at all. I could still get pregnant with one tube. Crappy results, but not calamitous.

We waited for the assigned date to consult with the obste-trician-gynecologist, an associate who worked with the clinic and would perform the surgery. Her earliest opening for the proce-dure was months away. I liked her; she was less alarmist than our first doctor.

"If you were trying this the old-fashioned way, you would never know if you had a blocked tube," she said, leafing through the countless pages on which I'd tracked months and months of the wax and wane of my ovulatory cycles. "You might get pregnant anyway."

"We could try while we wait for surgery?" I asked hopefully.

She shrugged. "Why not?" I took that and ran.

I was due to ovulate the next day and I called the fertility clinic. I said I wanted to make an insemination appointment. The nurse was not happy about that. I had to really work to convince her that the doctor we'd seen said it was okay to go ahead, yet even so, she remained stiff.

I figured it was about statistics — the clinic wants good pregnancy statistics and my HSG indicated I (possibly) couldn't offer that. But my body, my cycle charts; theoretically my choice. Not to mention we were paying for the procedure. I was determined to try.

I delivered their desired statistic: I got a positive pregnancy test after my first insemination. I stared at the plastic stick, stunned. I went for a confirmatory blood test and felt it was poetic justice that the nurse I'd argued with on the phone was the one who called to deliver the news about the "nicely positive pregnancy test."

I know I am one of few who gets this lucky. I have friends who tried month after month with no success, switching donors with the hope that it might help, or switching procedures to boost their chances. I feel grateful it went the way it did and have felt guilty sometimes within the tell-your-hell story circles where queer parents compare. Despite our journey for the right donor, it wasn't hell, and I recognize that.

I didn't experience my own Enormous Parenting Job worries until I was pregnant. I went from ecstatic to terrified within a few weeks: What was I thinking? How could I be a mother? The cells kept multiplying as I fretted and ate masses of Raisin Bran to ease my endless hunger and nausea. A friend who'd recently had a baby told me she had felt the same and got over it; I would too. I did, because I became too tired to worry.

I catnapped through pregnancy with my head on my desk in the afternoons. I loved feeling movement, from the early flutters to the determined bump of a heel moving under my skin from side to side. I grew to appreciate my maternity pants, and when I got pregnant a second time, I was into them the moment my regular pants were uncomfortable.

Labour was three days long as we transitioned from future parents to exhausted parents of a newborn. Our little sprite was tired too; she needed the help of oxygen to go from blue to blooming pink. When I felt those heels outside, pointed in my hands, it was truly amazing.

THE AUTHORITIES

"Come here," the border guard beckoned to our son, stepping a couple of feet away from us. Our four-year-old looked hesitantly at my partner, who moved to follow. He put up his hand to motion the rest of us to stay still.

"Where's your dad?" the guard asked our son.

"I don't have one."

"No? Then who's in charge?" the guard persisted.

Our son pointed at my partner and me: "They are."

We have done everything we can to protect the structure of the family we've created. Our children were born during a time when it wasn't a legal given that my partner would be recognized as a parent from birth, even though each child was considered and conceived while we were in our relationship, which predated the kids. Each of our kids was adopted by my partner (and adored by the lawyer, who sat them on her desk and offered toys from a basket as we signed paperwork), so we are both their legal parents.

When it became legal for queer couples to marry in Canada, we debated. We'd already had a commitment ceremony that served as our marriage; why do it again? We went back and forth, including discussions that ran the course from the history of marriage to whether we would change our names. We decided we would make it legal, this time a smaller event, and we called it a renewal of vows. We had a delighted flower girl and a ring bearer, who brought the rings in the scoop of his yellow front-end loader. I joke I've been married twice and never divorced.

The incident with the border guard who pulled our son aside wasn't the only time authorities have questioned our family, but it was the time I had to work the hardest not to blow a gasket. When the guard begrudgingly allowed us to pass, I wanted to scream at him for scaring our son. I didn't; I said, "Thank you" instead, once we were allowed to pass.

When we were trying to cross the border on another occasion, my partner was asked to produce the kids' passports (check), the adoption orders that prove our parentage (check) and proof there was no father on the scene. This comes in the form of a letter from the fertility clinic that indicates our kids were born with the help of an unknown donor (check). It is soft in its folds from use over many years, but it's a necessary thing to have and even then, he demanded my partner explain its meaning. The crowd behind us got a lesson in queer reproduction, a couple of times. I am sure that guard didn't want us to get through, but the fact that we produced all the requested documents and the line was lengthening behind us made it impossible for him to refuse.

We've had to spell out the structure of our family time and time again, even when it seems obvious to us and others, but not to whatever official is in front of us. When our daughter was ready for school, I went to fill out the forms and was met with utter puzzlement by the school secretary. She just couldn't see her way to two moms and no dad on the registration form.

"No father?" she asked.

"There are two moms. No father."

We went back and forth a bit over divorce (no), custody arrangements with a dad (again, no) for the audience of other parents filling out forms for their kids. She was clearly frazzled but accepted my form. The next day I got an apology call from the principal who explained that the woman I'd spoken with was a fill-in and not what we should anticipate at the school when our daughter arrived in the fall. I was grateful for that.

Overall, elementary school was great. Teachers were happy to meet us and include books about queer families like ours that we bought for their libraries. Parents were great, too (one told me she remembered me from the registration scene). If parents did have trouble with us, we never heard about it. Kids had no trouble at all. Our kids report they had one or two questions over the years, curiosity only.

My partner and I have always been publicly out and we knew that having children would require that at an even higher level. We made the choice to be involved at our kids' daycares and elementary school as much as we could. My partner worked on the school's parent advisory council and I had a flexible enough work schedule that I could put in a short volunteer shift one morning a week. We figured the more kids saw us as fixtures, the less Other we would seem. We were *here and queer*. Everyone *got used to it*.

THE LEAP

Who knows how life would have gone if we hadn't had kids? The choice to pursue parenthood and experience it in all its messy demands and rewards is one that has improved me. Of course, it's a decision you make without all the information you need, and once you have the information you need, you have kids. Ta-da! It's impossible that way. But in its impossibility, it is gritty, pure and true.

THE QUEER BABY PROJECT: EXCERPTS FROM THE EXPERIMENT[1]

Susan Meyers[2] and Kira Meyers-Guiden[3]

The following article contains excerpts from the ongoing longitudinal study of lesbian mothering conducted by the first author and endured by the second. The primary voice is that of the mother, Susan, with commentary by her daughter, Kira, who of course never asked to be born into this.

INTRODUCTION

SUSAN: It was the nineties, and all the lesbians were having children. Or so it seemed to us, whose lesbian friends had children from previous marriages, were adopting internationally or were getting pregnant through alternate fertilization (some involving helpful male friends and a turkey baster, others by going through a fertility clinic). Neither of us had thought about expanding our family at that point. I was busy developing my career and doing trauma work with abused kids, and my partner, Barb, was becoming a realtor while still doing a one-woman show as a country singer in all the honky-tonk bars in eastern Ontario. We had been together a couple of years and were enjoying building that relationship.

---

1. It is true that the title is somewhat ambiguous. Is this about queer parents or a queer baby? For the sake of clarity, it can be assumed both ways.

2 The first author, Susan Meyers, is a mother and a psychologist who has been associated with a university, a college, and a variety of children's mental health centres and has been in private practice and consultation work. She certainly never imagined herself to be a writer of anything other than scholarly articles.

3. The second author, Kira Meyers-Guiden, is certainly a writer but, since she is younger, a daughter and was tasked with doing all the difficult work of creating commentary and critique, has been relegated to secondary authorship.

So, what led us to our great experiment? Perhaps becoming more aware of kids in the lesbian families around us. Maybe my work treating kids from one of the largest sexual abuse investigations in Canada, where I got to spend my days working and playing with tenacious youngsters who were fighting hard just to be treated as kids. Maybe hearing our biological clocks ticking. Maybe Barb being from a boisterous Irish clan. Maybe it was all of these, or only some, or something else entirely that led us to start talking about having kids. But we did, and then I got to know more about Barb than I had in the past. She doesn't just talk about things; she gets them done. Our experiment had begun.

METHOD

Participants

Our queer baby project began with the two of us and then expanded to a wide variety of players: friends, family and the medical community (more to come on that part). We thought about adoption for a while, given my work with many kids who were in foster care. Then we talked about having a baby of our own and who would be the biological mom. I was pushing forty and am adopted myself without any idea of my genetic heritage. We found out that we were both categorized as potential "older mothers," even though Barb wasn't thirty-five yet. We read about the risks to the baby being born to "older moms," and we guessed that Barb was our best bet; she is also always the first one to jump into any project headlong and headstrong. So, we decided that we'd explore alternate fertilization with her as the mom to carry our baby. She talked to her family doctor one day and walked out with a referral to our local fertility clinic.

Materials and Procedure

Our trip to the clinic gave us an idea of what we might be up against as lesbian moms creating their own family. The first visit was during the fertility doctor's "clinic day," one of those days when everyone showed up in a large crowd and was then shut-tled off into tiny rooms for the five to ten minutes that the doctor could provide. Everything else was done by the nurses, medical students and residents of the teaching hospital. When Barb's name was called, we were ushered into a small room and provided with a hospital gown; we were told that the doctor would be in shortly.

Since we had indicated that we just wanted to consult the doctor about alternate fertilization, we weren't really sure what to do with the gown. Neither of us felt the need to put it on, and we studiously avoided looking at the stirrups on the exam table. We took turns sitting on the table, making that crinkly noise on the covering paper, since there was only one chair in the room, presumably soon to be occupied by the doctor. We made a list of what we wanted to ask, hopped on and off the table, and nervously awaited the person who could help us become a family.

Eventually the door opened, and a very efficient medical stu-dent entered with a clipboard and pen at the ready. We introduced ourselves as Barb and Susan; she seemed to feel that we could read her nametag. She looked at both of us (neither in a gown) and asked, "So, what is the problem?"

We both said, "No problem at all."

I said, "We want to talk about alternate fertilization."

She replied, "But what is the *problem*?"

Again, "No problem. We just want to talk about what is in-volved in alternate fertilization through your clinic."

"But what is the fertility problem?"

"We don't think there is a fertility problem. We want to talk about alternate fertilization to get pregnant."

"But what is the *problem* in getting pregnant?"

Sigh … So, I growled, "I have a *very* low sperm count!"

She immediately backed toward the door, spun around, clip-board clutched to her chest, and exited quickly without another question. We clearly saw who had the *problem*. We still wonder what that med student thought about her encounter with us that day. We hope she is still in medicine and maybe tells her students,

"When I was a med student, I learned a lot about listening to patients when I met these two women one day …"

The fertility doctor arrived quickly once the student had scurried off, and we agreed to meet him in his office so he could answer our questions about alternate fertilization, and so we could determine whether we wanted to pursue our dreams of a family with their clinic. After that meeting (where we informed him that yes, we did mind if he smoked his pipe), we decided to fully engage with the experimental procedure. We went to the compulsory appointments to assure the clinic that we were financially and psychologically stable, although we did choose our own social worker and psychiatrist to talk with. We found the experience to be a great way for us as prospective parents to start thinking about why we actually wanted to have a child, how our relationship would be affected and how we viewed ourselves as moms. Perhaps it's something that all soon-to-be parents should consider? Still, we weren't sure that this was the intended outcome of the required meetings. Mostly, we felt that we had cleared a couple of hurdles on the clinic's checklist.

We had to choose an anonymous sperm donor from a brief list of individuals identified by donor number, height, weight, hair and eye colour, and occupation. (The clinic gave us a list that had only white donors. We were sure that there were some donors from other racial groups — why weren't they on our list too?) We were assured that all sperm was screened for STIs and came from a reputable clinic in Montreal. (Would our HIV-negative baby have a propensity for French or English?) We wanted to pick someone with eye and hair colour similar to mine and we thought it was fitting that most of the donors were students, since I was a perennial student. "Not too tall and not too wide; that baby's got to come out of me," was Barb's concern. So, in the end, D-233 became my sperm stand-in. (Of course, we don't know if D-233 really had blue eyes and brown hair and was a student. Scary stories are out there about who actually provides sperm; luckily, none are out there about our clinic so far!)

We learned a lot about ovulation-monitoring and Barb became an expert in peeing on a stick to see if she was at the right point in her cycle for insemination. Each time the stick turned the right colour, we would have to rush off to the clinic. I would assiduously pay for a "straw" of D-233's sperm (thinking that this would look good if my role as a parent were ever questioned), and we'd go in together for the insemination. No candlelight, wine or sweet conversation — just fluorescent lights, a gown, scrunching along the crinkly paper, and stirrups. Nevertheless, there was exhilaration and anticipation … followed by a couple of letdowns when it didn't take. But, thanks to her lineage of fertile Irish women, the third time was the charm for Barb: we were pregnant!

KIRA: As a kid, my moms would read me *Heather Has Two Mommies* by Lesléa Newman. It's a sweet children's book about lesbian moms raising a kid. I identified a lot with Heather, and at the time it didn't seem strange that there was a book that paralleled my life. I thought all my friends in kindergarten were reading it. The first time I remember coming out as a queer spawn, I was shocked that the kids didn't get what I was telling them. Up until that point, my life experience seemed the same as everyone else's. I recall my friends and I talking about families when I was a toddler. Somehow, we got on the topic of artificial insemination. My friends had a lot of questions, and I was confused as to why they didn't already know about it. I have always known, and been proud of, my birth story. So, there's little old me at the ripe age of three explaining to the other tots that my mommies went to the doctor so they could pick out some sperm to put into my momma's vagina, so it could mix with her egg and make me. I wonder if my teacher overheard, and I wonder if any kids went home and explained to their nuclear families what the queer-baby told them. Regardless, this was the first of many times I've had to explain how I was made. Sometimes the story is met with, "Wow, that's so cool of your parents." Other times it is met with, "So you're a test-tube baby?" Mmm, not quite. Nevertheless, since then I've known that I am Other; that my family is "abnormal." (However, what family is normal if you think about it ...? But I digress.) I've known from a young age that all families are different, and that shared blood is not a necessity for a family.

RESULTS

SUSAN: It was a warm night in October. The federal election was in full swing, and Kim Campbell's Progressive Conservatives were slugging it out with Jean Chrétien's Liberals. The Toronto Blue Jays were slugging it out with the Philadelphia Phillies in game six of the World Series. A win that night could clinch the series, but the Blue Jays were down 6–5 in the bottom of the ninth. And yet — Joe Carter stepped up to the plate and hit a home run that drove in three runs for the win, and the series. We jumped to our feet, cheered and danced, and Barb said, "I think I peed myself ..."

It wasn't pee: her water broke — sort of. So began days of minor contractions and calls to our birth coach. Was this really happening? We were finally going to see that little person that we had been talking to, singing to and hoping for all that time. When we went to the obstetrician on Monday, she was horrified that Barb's water broke on Saturday and we didn't call. Didn't we know the risk of infection increases once the amniotic sac was broken? (No.) The obstetrician decided to induce immediately. Off we went to the birthing room, calling our birth coach to come right away. Barb quickly got to know what contractions really were like. Our visions of a quiet birth with just our coach and us, with a quick visit from the obstetrician for delivery, quickly began to morph into something else: monitors for Barb, a fetal monitor for the baby, IVs for the induction and many long hours of waiting for Barb's cervix to dilate as she was having strong contractions. We called Barb's mom in Toronto to say that Barb had been induced and she would be a grandma in a while, and we promised to call once things began to progress more. We called back to find that she wasn't there and had already headed for the train station.

Many more hours of pain for Barb; many trips for me to the breakroom to get ice chips and catch the election on TV. The Progressive Conservatives were getting trounced by the Liberals; Barb was getting trounced by contractions and little dilation. The plan for a drug-free birth gave way for the relief of an epidural ("How come they never said how great this is? I don't care that I can't feel my legs; this is good!"); an intimate birth gave way for a series of doctors, residents and med students ("Is it alright if I examine you?" they would ask, to which Barb would cry out, "As long as you *don't hurt me!*"). Barb drifted in and out of tired sleep. I was wide awake, battling instant insomnia as soon as the monitors bleeped. I soon heard the tap of high heels on the hospital linoleum and the squeak of a rolling suitcase as my mom-in-law arrived in the middle of the night. ("Bejesus, it's happening!" she murmured in the loudest stage whisper.) I settled her on the cot for a sleep and soon there was a pattern of loud snores, which scared the nurse who checked the monitors.

Finally, in the wee hours of the morning, dilation had progressed. The chief resident began to help with the delivery. Birth coach, mom-in-law and I held Barb's hands and helped her breathe while she pushed. And pushed and pushed. ("Isn't the baby supposed to be coming soon? It didn't happen like this in the movie …") With each push, it seemed like more medical staff arrived. I could swear the housekeeping staff was there, and someone was selling tickets to the birth. The head of obstetrics arrived (our fertility doctor) and started talking about forceps and a C-section. Barb simply said, "Get this baby OUT!"

The resident remained calm, tried to turn the baby a bit more and finally used the forceps. Amazingly, out slid our daughter! A girl! We had expected a boy although we had asked for the gender to be a secret until birth. Is it an old lesbian tale or are there actually more boys born through alternate fertilization? In fact, we were so sure we were having a boy we hadn't picked out any girls' names. The baby, who we later called Kira, didn't make the usual hearty cry of a newborn — it was more of a grunting noise — and was taken over to be suctioned by one of the doctors. We all cried tears of joy and relief.

The medical staff then said they had to take our just-new baby to the neonatal intensive care unit (NICU). The risk of infection was high since Barb's water broke so long before she was born (damn Joe Carter and his homerun!), and she had a bit of trouble breathing. Someone from NICU was on their way. A nurse arrived in scrubs with a light-up jack-o-lantern pin on her uniform (it was almost Halloween) and bundled our baby up; I said I would go with her. Barb, fully feeling her load of drugs and the relief of having given birth, was busy hitting on the chief resident ("Shawna, what a nice name…") as we breezed out of the room. As we hastily moved along the hospital corridors, the nurse asked, "So, you are the grandmother?" *Oh my god*, I thought. *I've just turned forty and just become a mom for the first time — do I look like a grandmother?*

"No, I'm the other mother."

"The other mother?"

"Yes, my partner, Barb, is the mother, and I'm the other mother."

"Right! The other mother."

"And you're a nurse in NICU"

"Yes, I work in NICU. But I'm a neonatologist."

"Oh, right. The neonatologist."

By the time we swung through the doors of NICU with my daughter Kira, we had both sorted out our stereotypes and were ready to sort out how Kira was doing. Luckily, fears that she might have meningitis or a serious infection were dispelled within a few hours, and she settled quickly into her incubator, looking like a seven-pound giant among her nursery-mates who, for the most part, were much smaller and sicker than she was. Barb got some much-needed rest from the lengthy labour as I stayed with our daughter until she could join Barb and her grandma. Everyone in NICU knew I was her mom, and I learned to respect the hard work of all the staff members there, neonatologists included.

DISCUSSION

So, the first part of the queer baby project was a success: we managed to add a wonderful daughter to our lesbian family. However, we soon found out that not everyone considered us a family. At the hospital, we filled in the Statement of Live Birth to register Kira's birth. Under the section for parents, Barb put her information under Mother, and I scratched out the Father heading and titled it Partner (Other Mother), where I filled out my information. We sent it off to the Vital Statistics office in Kingston, Ontario.

As we settled into our new life of sleep deprivation and learning how to be parents, we received a phone call from the City of Kingston, which indicated that they couldn't register Kira's birth. She needed to be registered under her biological parents. We explained that we had gone to the fertility clinic and that there wasn't a father, just an anonymous sperm donor, with Barb as the birth mother. Kira had two parents: Barb and me. They replied that they couldn't send on the information to the provincial department of Vital Statistics because the form was filled in incorrectly. We politely asked them to send it to the provincial department anyway. Glad to have it off their desk, they agreed to send it, and let us know that we would be hearing from the province shortly.

KIRA: Growing up, Mother's Day was a big deal in my house. (As you can imagine, with two moms I had to make double the PB&J breakfast sandwiches — which I made on the floor). Alternatively, Father's Day was just another day. However, when you're in elementary school teachers like to have kids craft for these days. When I was in grade four, my teacher told us to bring in one of our dad's old ties so that we could create a piece of artwork for Father's Day. When I told my moms this, they either scavenged the house or made a quick trip to Value Village, because when the crafting day came upon us, I had a tie to bring to class. I decided to make this art for my grandad. I would call my grandad each Father's Day, and every summer I would go to Grandad Camp; he acted as my "father figure."

Fast forward fourteen years later to me announcing to my grandad that I am getting married to my long-time female partner (who he has met multiple times, I might add). He responds that I am no longer his "best girl." After a few pointed phone calls, where he told me that he didn't agree with what I do but still wanted to be a part of my life (just not the gay part), and me telling him he's a homophobic jerk, we are now no longer speaking. I was flabbergasted: I have grown up with this man, who has been a part of his lesbian daughter, her partner and their kid's life for as long as I have been alive; yet, as soon as the queer spawn identifies as queer, we are an abomination. One of the main reasons I have decided to kick him out of my life is because he said that he knew the children of lesbians would continue this shameful lifestyle. He can insult and misunderstand me all he wants, but he can't give my parents trouble for raising me. My queerness is my own and is not a negative reflection of my moms. If anything, they provided me with a household where I could be myself without judgment. So, goodbye homophobic Grandad, and goodbye Father's Day along with him.

SUSAN: It was a Friday night, and I was working late at the children's mental health centre. My phone rang, and the person on the line identified himself as the deputy minister of Vital Statistics of the Province of Ontario. (I think he was hoping to leave a voicemail!) He informed me that he was not able to register Kira's birth as he could not list me as her parent under the Vital Statistics Act, since I wasn't her biological parent. I noted that I wasn't sure why a child's birth certificate had to have biological parents listed, since the fertility clinic that we had used had a stipulation that heterosexual couples who used their services could indicate on the Statement of Live Birth that they were the parents, regardless of their biological link. Fathers who weren't biological fathers put their names down and were accepted by the province as parents. Was the province conducting paternity and maternity tests before issuing birth certificates? He admitted that they were not, but noted that these were unusually rare cases. (This of course doesn't include the usual rates of 5 to 15 percent of fathers who aren't aware that their offspring aren't their biological children.) Our conversation became a bit less civil after that, especially after his imputations that the fabric of society might unravel if anyone could willy-nilly call themselves a parent. (I reimbursed my agency for the phone that cracked when I slammed it down that evening.)

So, we looked at other ways that I could legally be Kira's mom. Socially, there was no problem with me being her mom, except for the occasional mishap of being thought to be her grandparent. Our friends and families were thrilled with her and treated us both as moms (Mommy and Momma), but we worried about what would happen if something happened to Barb; I wouldn't be able to make legal or medical decisions for Kira. I might not be able to travel with her — or even be with her if someone with a stronger biological tie wanted to parent her. All these things that we didn't think of when we began our great experiment!

KIRA: When I was a kid I did gymnastics. My mom Susan would usually take me to my gymnastics since it was at 6 p.m. on Mondays, and Barb was almost always still working. I loved gymnastics, but the reason I stopped was because of the people I was training with. I wasn't a tall, slim, popular girl; instead I was short and stout and just wanted to do as many cartwheels in a row as possible. Apparently, my fellow gymnasts' distaste for me travelled upstairs in the viewing area toward my mother. Susan discovered that the girls learned to make fun of my weight from their moms. My mothers' queerness, I imagine, also sparked some tension.

One day I was getting changed in the change room and one kid kept asking me, referring to my mom, "Who's that?" Barb was at the gym the previous week, which had sparked the sudden interest in my parents. Good thing I was learning about Kelso's Choice in school! (Kelso is a big green frog that teaches kids strategies to resolve conflict. Check him out, he's a cool dude.) So, I practised my newly learned Kelso's Choice and ignored her, but she kept pushing. She followed me out of the change room, pointed to my mom and loudly asked, so that all my peers (and my poor mother) could hear, "Who's that?!"

Storming out of the gym, I responded, "MY GRANDMA!" I will never forget the look on my mom's face. This is one of the first times that I learned I should be ashamed of my family and that queerness is something to hide.

My mother, being an amazing person, laughed it off as she played with me and tried to figure out why I'd said what I'd said. However, being a queer person myself, I can only imagine the pain that I caused her to think that her own kid was ashamed of her. (I don't remember if what I experienced that day was shame, annoyance or confusion, but whatever it was, I'm sure it didn't feel good for my mom). I've now learned that Susan was mistaken as my grandparent since the birthing room, so this wasn't anything new to her, but I still feel bad. Kids can internalize shame even if that language is never thrown at them; it's the way that you're treated, talked about and seen by others that teaches kids, even at the ripe age of six, that you should call your queer mom your grandma so you don't have to explain alternative fertilization for a fifth time that week. It felt like I was constantly coming out as queer spawn, but that one time I just wanted to stay in the closet.

SUSAN: It was 1994, and things were pretty bleak for non-biological lesbian parents. Nonetheless, we began a mission to ensure that I, as a non-biological parent, was considered a parent in the eyes of the law in Ontario. It wasn't 2003, when the first same-sex marriage cases were triumphant in Ontario. It wasn't 2005, when Canada joined the ranks of countries allowing same-sex marriage. It wasn't 2007 yet, either, when an Ontario superior court judge ruled that couples who use anonymous sperm donors should enjoy the same rights as those who conceive "naturally" (although the judge left out those whose donor was known to them). And it wasn't January 2017, when the All Families Are Equal Act was proclaimed in Ontario, ensuring that same-sex parents who use a sperm or egg donor or surrogate are legally recognized as parents.

KIRA: A couple years ago, a co-worker asked what my parents do for work. I responded, "My one mom is a real estate agent, and my other mom is a psychologist for kids' mental health." Silence. Great. I quickly asked, "What about your parents?"

"My dad does this, and my mom does that."

"Cool." A couple minutes went by, and I could tell she was trying to work something out in her head. Something like, One mom + one mom = no dad? But where is Dad? Did Dad die? Is there a stepmom? How can there be two moms?

And then the inevitable question happened: "I'm sorry, I don't mean to be rude, and please don't take this the wrong way. You don't have to answer if you don't want to."

Just spit it out, I thought.

"So, you have two moms? Or your dad is the psychologist, right?"

"Yeah, no, I have two moms."

"Where's your dad?"

"I don't have one."

"Oh." She looked at me with such pity. At that point I began to feel bad; I didn't want her to think one of my parents had died, so I launched into the next explanation.

"I have two moms. They are lesbian. It's always been that way."

"Oh, I see. Cool!"

"Yup."

"But wait ... who's your real mom?"

Halt. I will explain to someone until I'm blue in the face the many different ways different bodies can have babies, but I am a lot less patient when one starts to peg one of my mothers' motherhood as invalid.

"What do you mean?"

She squirmed. "I mean, which one is the real one, like, you know ..."

"Sorry, what are you saying?"

She began to sweat. "Like, which one had you?"

"They both did. They are both my mom."

She was visually sweaty, squirming and now confused. "But ... how does that work?"

I started to feel bad for the little lamb. It was obvious she was questioning everything she ever knew about the vagina and was thinking I was an alien, so I put her out of her misery.

"Oh, do you mean which one birthed me?"

Sweet relief. She made an audible sigh.

"My mom did."

The confusion set back in all over again. Sometimes I'll tell someone which one actually birthed me, but I get the sense that they feel my other mother is less of a mom because of that. Also, I never ask people with parents who pass as heterosexual who birthed the kids because dads can also become pregnant. (Personal service announcement: Trans people exist!) But I digress.

SUSAN: We took the only route, which had been opened up by a few brave lesbian parents in Ontario who had used the court to ensure that both parents were legally viewed as such (not just having both their names on the birth certificate). They had petitioned their family courts to use adoption measures, like those often used by heterosexual step-parents, to grant legal parenthood to the non-biological mom. So, off we went to court to adopt our own daughter. We jumped through the hoops of having to see the social worker at the Frontenac Children's Aid Society, where Barb was given the social worker's card, "just in case you change your mind about giving her up for adoption," and going through a cursory home study. In 1995, we finally attended the Unified Family Court in Kingston (having paid a few thousand dollars to a lawyer), and we were granted the privilege of both becoming the legal parents of our daughter.

It is now 2018, and the experiment is still ongoing. Data has already been collected for the school years (preschool through university), the transition to young adulthood (for the child) and mature years (for the parents), and marriage (for both parents and child). Analysis is ongoing. Future excerpts may be published as they become available.

Best Laid Plans

Sara Graefe

Our early attempts to get pregnant were sensual, softly lit affairs. If there *is* a fertility goddess, we wanted to make sure she was paying attention. Amanda and I held hands and gazed into each other's eyes, Israel Kamakawiwo'ole's Hawaiian rendition of "Twinkle, Twinkle Little Star" lapping through shared ear buds. We imagined ourselves on the Maui beach from our honeymoon or under soft sheets in our own bedroom, wishing away the clinical examination table, the crinkly blue hospital paper, my feet up in stirrups. We drew slow, deep breaths together, *in and out*, as the clinic nurse threaded the catheter tip up through my vagina and into my cervix. As the nurse pushed the plunger, inseminating me with our donor's sperm, Amanda and I kissed, consciously inviting a baby to share in this, our beautiful life together. After the nurse cleaned up and discreetly left the room, Amanda brought me off gently with her hand, the orgasm rocking my body and reclaiming the clinical procedure as an act of love.

Maybe it was all a tad too precious. Two weeks later, my period would inevitably arrive and we'd be reduced to teary, irritable messes, convinced that we'd never be able to conceive in a million years — until the next cycle, when our hope was rekindled. They don't call it the fertility roller coaster for nothing.

Paradoxically, the cycle I finally got pregnant during was a total gong show. When we picked up our sperm, specially thawed and washed for the intrauterine insemination (IUI), the clinic lab technician quickly verified the donor number on the tiny vial, thrust it into my hand and abruptly closed the door without wishing me good luck. On previous attempts, the lab workers had always wished us good luck. It felt like a bad omen.

Then, in the insemination room, I'd barely got my undies off and feet up in stirrups when not one, but two nurses barged through the door, so engrossed in idle chit-chat that they barely acknowledged us. We'd been doing this long enough to know the standard clinic protocol, and this definitely was not it.

Amanda and I exchanged a pained glance. I was always a bundle of nerves before an IUI, and this wasn't helping. To make matters worse, one of them was a dead-ringer for an ex-girlfriend I'd left on not-so-great terms, from her short mousy hair right down to her thick New Zealand accent — the last person I wanted in the room as Amanda and I tried to make a baby. The nurses must have caught our look because they finally stopped talking.

"There are going to be two of us today," the Kiwi announced brightly, turning toward us. She indicated her co-worker, a fresh-faced young Asian woman. "This is her first time, and I'm here to walk her through it."

I wasn't sure what was worse — that my ex's doppelganger was going to hang around and stare up my vagina as her colleague pushed the plunger, or that I was going to be inseminated by a first-timer. We could have saved ourselves the two hundred bucks we'd forked out to have the job done by a seasoned professional (on top of the seven hundred fifty dollars a squirt for the donor sperm) and given it a whirl at home with the turkey baster.

"Don't worry," the Kiwi nurse continued, half to me, half to her colleague. "First time lucky, right?"

"I'll try my best." The young nurse shot me a reassuring smile as she gently inserted the duck lips. Her delicate touch and gentle bedside manner immediately calmed me down. She could do my pap smear any day.

This was only our third cycle, but the pressure was on. If it didn't take, my reproductive endocrinologist wanted me to undergo laparoscopic surgery to investigate the possibility of endometriosis, something I desperately hoped to avoid. It seemed preposterous, anyway: What straight couple trying in the privacy of their own bedroom rushes out for surgery if they're not pregnant yet, after three short months? But as a queer couple, we were paying through the nose for these clinical inseminations, and the doctor didn't want to waste our time or money.

The young nurse was now oh-so-gently threading the catheter tip up through my vagina. She really did have the magic touch. I tried to breathe and relax into the procedure, but her colleague wouldn't shut up. As Amanda held my hand and gazed lovingly into my eyes, my ex's evil twin kept peppering us with questions, some relevant — "How many cycles have you been trying?" — but mostly none of her business — "Which sperm bank did you use?" "How did you decide who was going to carry?" and "Do you care if it's a boy or a girl?" — all while coaching her trainee through the insemination process: "You just kinda feel your way up to the cervix ..."

I tried to focus on my breathing, both to tune her out and to take my mind off the intense discomfort I was now feeling in my pelvic area. But just as the young nurse located my cervix and inserted the catheter, the Kiwi began filling her in about pain and how this procedure didn't hurt. I gritted my teeth. *What the fuck was she talking about?* On an earlier attempt, I'd had the most awful cramping as the catheter went in. I must have said something out loud, because the Kiwi turned to me with a whole new slew of questions and a mini-seminar on the nature of the pain I'd experienced.

"I — I'd rather not discuss it just now," I managed finally, just as her colleague fast-tracked our donor's semen into my cervix with the syringe.

For a pregnancy that had been so meticulously planned, it was the most unromantic conception imaginable. As we hurried to the car to get back to work, half-laughing, half-cringing at how awful it had been, I convinced myself that this time, it definitely wouldn't take. I was already half-wishing my period would hurry up and come early so we could start again, clean slate.

"Wouldn't it be ironic if I did get pregnant this time?" I quipped. "And we have to think back on *this* as the moment of our child's conception?"

"If you get pregnant this time," Amanda grinned, "then none of this will matter."

Motherhood was something Amanda and I had both wanted for a long time. Before we'd met in our mid-thirties, I'd consciously taken time out from intimate relationships to get my shit together. During that long, dry spell, my ticking biological clock had gone on overdrive and I'd started investigating planned single motherhood, just in case. Amanda, meanwhile, had tried to conceive with a previous long-term partner, inseminating with sperm donated by her lover's gay brother. The first and only attempt didn't take, something she'd had to grieve along with the eventual demise of that relationship.

On our very first date, I spotted a pink, sparkly princess wand on the back seat of Amanda's car, not exactly in keeping with her butchy style. "I'm playing fairy godmother at my friend's daughter's birthday party," she explained, blushing madly. Already flying high on pheromones and endorphins, I felt my heart skip another beat — she likes kids.

It was 2004 and equal marriage legislation had newly passed in some parts of the country, including our home province of BC. A celebratory feeling lingered in the air, the sense that anything was now possible. Queer couples young and old were flocking to get married, many re-affirming relationships spanning decades. Others in the community were steadfastly choosing not to get hitched, but at least *we now had a choice*. The gayby boom was raging, thanks to advances not only in LGBTQ2 rights but also in assisted reproductive technologies, making it easier than ever for queers to conceive.

So much had changed in a single decade. When I first came out in the late eighties and early nineties, it was unfathomable that I would be able to get married during my lifetime. While planned lesbian parenthood certainly existed, it was so underground that it was completely off my radar. The only queer moms I knew were older lesbian couples who'd had kids in previous, straight relationships. Kissing my first girlfriend meant kissing motherhood goodbye, or so I'd thought at the time.

My older cousin was much savvier. "Sara can still have kids," she'd famously told my aunt, trying to explain why my coming out wasn't the tragedy the rest of the family seemed to think it was. "Nothing's wrong with her womb. And now there will be two wombs."

That's what Amanda and I had naively believed, too, when we first embarked on our baby-making journey. Lesson number one: don't make any assumptions and be prepared for ever-shifting expectations. Amanda was only thirty-five when we first met but already having irregular periods and hot flashes. She was mortified when our family doctor referred her to a seminar on menopause. She was the only woman in the room under fifty, not to mention the only queer. When people ask how we chose who was going to gestate, Amanda will point to her butchy frame and joke, "Me? Go through the physical rigours of pregnancy?" In truth, I was the only one with a viable womb; I ended up being the one to conceive, more by default than anything else.

One decision down, a zillion left to go. We still had to figure out how to get our hands on that slippery, elusive sperm. The choices we faced getting the goods seemed daunting and all consuming. Fresh or frozen? Known or unknown donor? Would we try first at home, or go straight to the clinic? Should we opt for the cheapest, easiest scenario, the one where we retained the most control? Or the one that seemed most likely to get us pregnant — whatever that was?

At the beginning, we were dead-set on a known donor and even toyed with the idea of inseminating with fresh sperm at home. We not only wanted our donor to be someone we knew, but also a person who would be a part of our child's life, a kind of uncle figure. The problem was, there weren't many guys in our dyke-centered lives. My mind raced back through time, making an inventory of every man I'd ever been close to, from the gay boy I'd dated in high school to guys I'd slept with during university as I'd tried to make sense of my emerging sexuality. Could I really call them up after all these years and say, "Hey, how's it going? And by the way, care to donate some sperm?"

The natural candidate seemed to be Amanda's best friend Nigel, a flamboyant gay man she'd met at theatre school in England. They had been the only two queers in the program and had gravitated toward each other like moths to a flame, becoming instant friends. Nigel was someone who lived large and with intense passion; every second word out his mouth was "Brilliant!" or "Fantastic!" It was impossible not to have a good time when he was around. They'd stayed in each other's lives well beyond university and even after Amanda's move to Canada. Nigel had immediately warmed to me and was best man at our wedding. When we oh-so-tentatively broached the donor subject with him, he was not only open to the idea but also flattered and profoundly touched. Yes, he'd be delighted to play the role of queer uncle and no, he wasn't at all interested in co-parenting. It was perfect.

However, as we began to investigate the possibility more seriously, we encountered stumbling block after stumbling block. There was the simple question of geography: Nigel still lived in the UK, so using fresh sperm each cycle was out of the question. Even if we went the frozen route, how would we possibly collect enough for multiple inseminations if he were only able to visit Vancouver once a year? Like many gay guys, Nigel liked to sleep around. As sex-positive queers, Amanda and I didn't have an issue with this per se, but it did mean we'd have to address the touchy issue of a quarantine period with him, as well as the barrage of tests he'd have to undergo to ensure he was clean and HIV negative. We suddenly found ourselves questioning everything: Nigel looks nothing like Amanda — does that matter? What about his history of clinical depression? What if he changes his mind about being an uncle and wants custody rights, like Michael's character on *Queer As Folk*?

Maybe, we realized, we were more in love with the *idea* of using a known donor than the actuality. Maybe what we were really looking for was frozen sperm from an anonymous donor — provided we could find someone open to later contact. Amanda and I had both worked in the adoption field, Amanda as a social worker and me as researcher, and the parallels between using anonymous donor sperm and closed adoption weren't lost on us. We knew our child would grow up wondering about their donor and where they came from. At the very least, we wanted to give our kid the option to have contact with their donor dad after they turned eighteen, rather than closing that door before they were even conceived.

While we felt good about our decision, it immediately limited our options, both in terms of which sperm bank we could use and the range of donors available. The new Assisted Human Reproduction Act had recently passed in Canada, meaning cryobanks could no longer pay sperm donors for their goods and services. During the transition period after the proclamation of the new legislation, our clinic only sourced open ID donors from their US supplier, a cryobank in Atlanta that, if the jokes around our local LGBT parenting community are any indication, almost single-handedly fuelled the Canadian gayby boom in the mid-2000s. The other downside to using an anonymous donor was that it was going to cost us a lot more money to get pregnant than we'd originally budgeted, before even factoring in the premium for open ID sperm.

In a bittersweet twist of fate, I'd lost my favourite uncle to a stroke the very month before Amanda came into my life. A cultured British gentleman, Uncle Michael had come of age when homosexuality was illegal (think Alan Turing) and had lived out his days as a bachelor. Never having children of his own, he'd doted on his many nieces and nephews. My brother and I have fond memories of zooming through the English countryside with my uncle in his blue MG convertible, wind sweeping through our hair. He'd taught me how to play solitaire and gently nurtured my appreciation for gourmet cooking and classical music. His death was a profound loss on many levels. I grieved not only his sudden passing but also the fact he'd never been able to love openly. In parting, however, he also left a huge gift — an inheritance split equally between his nieces and nephews. It was both a surprise and a tremendous privilege. My portion became our sperm money. Even though it had been impossible for my uncle to come out in his own life, I was pretty sure, given his love of kids, that he'd approve of our queer baby-making project.

The next challenge was choosing an anonymous sperm donor. We were a tad daunted when we first logged onto the cryobank's website and found ourselves faced with hundreds of options. But once we'd entered our basic criteria — that we were looking for an open ID donor who was Canadian compliant, meaning his American-approved sperm had passed the extra, rigorous tests required by Health Canada — the list of eligible donors shrank down to a more manageable thirty. As we zeroed in on donors with a similar physical appearance and cultural background to Amanda, we were down to eight possible contenders and began to worry about the opposite problem: slim pickings.

To get more information, we had to shell out a couple hundred bucks for the privilege of viewing the full donor profiles. As we were beginning to discover, the more badly you wanted something in this process, the more you had to pay. So, we held our noses and entered our credit card info. Up popped personal specs on each donor, a sample baby and adult photo, pertinent medical info, detailed parental, maternal and sibling family histories, and a self-assessed personality profile. There was a lot to absorb, but these extended profiles started to give us a sense of these donors as living, breathing people, as opposed to a faceless number. But whom were we going to choose? Online shopping for half of your child's genetic material isn't exactly like ordering from Amazon, where you can always send stuff back if you're not satisfied.

Each profile also included a personal essay, which was ultimately the clincher. As a writer, I'm always a sucker for a good essay, but in this case, it went well beyond that — the donors' personalities really shone through on the page. Many guys who'd looked good in their profile completely bombed in the essay department. Some would say things along the lines of "Actually, I just needed some extra cash to get through school." While we applauded these guys for their honesty and resourcefulness, this wasn't necessarily the type of statement Amanda and I wanted to show our kid when they started asking questions about their donor.

Others used their essay to frame their jerking off into a cup as a noble act of charity, which was all well and good, except the language was often unfortunate: "I just want to help all those poor, infertile mothers and fathers out there." Even though I hadn't yet experienced infertility, the phrasing made me wince (at least they hadn't said "barren"). Not only that, but we were completely off their radar as a fertile queer couple. Was this someone our child could contact at eighteen and talk with freely about growing up in a family with two moms? Hard to gauge, and we didn't want to risk it.

Worse yet, a surprising number of essays exposed the writers as evangelical Christians. Initial sentiments of charity would quickly balloon into full-blown sermons as the donor seized the opportunity to preach the word of God to their potential offspring. Presumably not folk who'd welcome contact from our child down the road, other than to "save" them from their "sinful" upbringing.

Then came the young family doctor who had been an honour student (as I had been) and a successful athlete (like Amanda). His baby photo was adorable, and his adult photo confirmed that he'd grown up to be a handsome man. He had similar features and colouring to Amanda and, bonus, he even had dimples. Amanda had fallen for mine the moment we'd first met, when I'd flashed her a shy smile at a cheesy LGBT speed-dating event. "I hope our kids have dimples too," she used to whisper as we cuddled in bed, her finger tracing the tiny indentation in my cheek. If our donor had dimples, she'd be doubling her odds.

The doctor donor was also a mix of Amanda's and my cultural backgrounds. In both the formal personality tests and in his responses to the more general social/lifestyle questions, he came across as a lovely, gentle, thoughtful man, an extroverted introvert who worked hard and was highly motivated, both in his career and recreational pursuits. Someone who was *not* donating sperm for God (thank goodness), but, as he put it, in the same spirit with which he donated blood to the Red Cross. All in all, someone not unlike us: an engaging, liberal-minded person we'd probably enjoy having over for dinner. His essay sealed the deal: "If you are reading this," he started, "you no doubt have quite an interesting relationship with me, which may or may not be easy to accept."

We were so surprised that we had to re-read that first sentence multiple times. He was actually addressing the child in the first person! He clearly understood that this kid would have tons of questions about their origins and would be reading these very words down the road. No other donor we'd encountered so far had thought to do this.

"Some of what I will tell you may make this acceptance more difficult, but it is important to what I am and by extension, what your background is."

He totally got the complexity of his role as anonymous donor and of his unusual relationship with our potential child. He went on to talk about what an inspiration and role model his own father has been. He outlined a few key principles he'd learned from his dad, values that have guided his life and that very much meshed with our own — everything from the importance of education, working hard and keeping your eye on your goals, to eating your vegetables and remembering to smile because it has a wonderful effect on people. He called himself a bit of a goof, talked about his love of animals and the outdoors, his appreciation for all kinds of music even though he can't carry a tune, and his passion for sports, too many to list.

In closing, he wrote, "The fact that your parents cared enough and wanted to have you badly enough to go to the extent they did is very special indeed. This is leaps and bounds further toward being your parents than anything I have done. I hope for the very best for you in life and you will certainly make your parents proud."

Bingo, we'd found our donor. Dr. Boy, we affectionately dubbed him, because he was so much younger than us and still so boyish in his adult photo. How could he possibly be old enough to practice medicine?

We'd been warned by our clinic to pick at least three different candidates, in case our first choice wasn't available. Dr. Boy was a hard act to follow, but we came up with two others we felt we could live with. Lucky for us, our dream donor had units in stock when the nurse phoned in the order. Within a few weeks, six units of Dr. Boy's sperm were on ice at our fertility clinic and our insemination dance began.

We only had to try for three cycles. Two weeks after that cringeworthy insemination, I peed on a stick and, to my amazement, discovered I was pregnant. Not only did I dodge the dreaded laparoscopic surgery, but nine months later I gave birth to a beautiful baby boy.

Amanda was right. As soon as I was pregnant, our less-than-ideal conception didn't really matter anymore, nor did the angst we'd experienced over what had felt like life and death decisions — known or unknown donor? Fresh or frozen sperm? We were having a baby!

These things matter even less now that our son's actually here, a living, breathing person in his own right. His first words were "Mom-mom," meaning Mommy, for me, "Mama," for his Mama Manda and, instead of "Dada," "daag," for our two black pugs. He's got blond hair and blue eyes like both his moms, as well as the dimples that Amanda special-ordered. He has his donor's skin tone, which is more like Amanda's than mine, and he's unconsciously picked up her facial expressions, so much so that we often keep people guessing about which of us is his birth mother. Now ten, he's a kind, gentle, self-proclaimed tomgirl who loves to read and draw comics. His middle name is "Michael" after my late, closeted uncle, whose generous inheritance covered our baby-making costs.

I didn't fully appreciate how lucky we were in our conception journey until we tried for a second child. We loved our kid so much that of course we wanted another. We braved through three years of fruitless IUI cycles and a failed attempt at in vitro fertilization, including a mad scramble to find a new donor when Dr. Boy retired. There was also the costly, time-consuming transfer to a new clinic after the abrupt closure, mid-cycle, of our long-standing hospital facility. We finally walked away with nothing to show for our efforts but a mountain of debt and an even bigger mountain of grief.

Our son may not have a sibling, but he has no question about how he came into the world. He was in the room with Amanda and me for countless IUIs over those three difficult years, including repeat visits with the infamous Kiwi nurse, those months I surged early or on a weekend and we couldn't snag last-minute childcare. At four years of age, at the height of our trying for number two, he made a passionate, expressive painting in art class that he told the teacher to title, "Mommy and Mama Going to the Hospital to Make a Baby." He proudly showed off his masterpiece at home, pointing out the fact that Amanda and I were both smiling because he was the baby we were about to create and this made us so happy.

"Yes," we affirmed, fighting back tears and pulling him into a three-way hug. "We love you so much."

Don't make any assumptions and be prepared for ever-shifting expectations. In the end, we're the queer family of three that we were meant to be.

Pathway

Patrice Leung

It's unnatural. This motherhood thing. I'm a much better dad. The forager-hunter part of my atavistic brain is big and strong. I can put a roof over my children's heads. Bring home the bacon. Rule the roost. I am a Great Provider.

I run movie sets, from low-budget Canadian indies to bloated multimillion-dollar American behemoths. They call me AD, the assistant director. I help the director achieve his (rarely her) artistic vision while organizing the day-to-day machinations of the set. I manage white, straight men (mostly still). They follow me into battle. Each day I lead them to the other side of twelve, sometimes sixteen or eighteen, hours on the most efficient path possible. Hopefully, we all emerge not too scathed. It is my job to have a plan B, C and X when A falls through (Damn weather! Damn actors!). I must keep the army moving. The challenges of each show sometime scare, but do not cower, me. I embrace them. Revel in their intensity. Thrive on each degree of difficulty.

And yet. Two little orphan Chinese girls. My daughters, Keala and Tasia. They terrify the shit out of me. Bring my ego to its knees. School me in the depth of my flaws.

Oh yeah. This motherhood thing. It is hard.

It's not as if I wasn't warned.

My dad passed away when I was thirty-seven. James Ethelbert Leung. A man who absorbed life's tempests and just got on with it. He was the panda to my mother's tiger. He always made me feel capable. And he championed my butchness.

"Trice is good at whatever sport she tries," he said, his Trinidadian cadences singing out to his friends at the second tee of the pitch and putt in Stanley Park. "Her shoulders are muscular from delivering newspapers."

He was an inveterate punster. Of the "two Wongs don't make a White" variety. When he died, I, theretofore a career dyke, thought to myself, "My child will never hear his stupid puns." It was that twinge that set me down the slippery slope to parenthood.

"Ma, I'm thinking of adopting."

I was sitting in the kitchen of my widowed mother's Vancouver Special, with its matching avocado fridge and stove. My mother was ironing, as I knew she would be. It was Saturday after all. Always the best time for me to proclaim anything, as she was anchored to the ironing board.

She glanced up briefly from the towel she was creasing to perfection, and then looked back down.

"Parenting is hard," she said.

And there it was: the warning shot across my bow.

I could just imagine the right-wing evangelical tenets swirling around her vocal cords.

"You're not even married. Children need a mother and a father. Homosexual abominations should not be allowed to have children. You are a lesbian. Conclusion?"

But she said nothing more. Nor did I. In our family, the superficial saved us from having to face messy emotions. Inside, however, I was screaming, "I want my child to know you before you die!"

Aii ya! Stockholm Syndrome. With an Asian flair. My mother, Grace Ahoy Leung, all five feet of her, was my most profound influence. She combined a brutal style of parenting with a fierce love for all three of her children. She was a tsunami of will, discipline, intelligence and compassion. Her personality loomed too large for mere reminiscences. She had to be experienced to be believed. She was seventy-nine. Time was a-ticking.

"Why do you want to adopt?" asked the social worker.

She was a very nice, non-judgmental white woman, dispatched by my adoption agency. I'll call her C.

C and I were sitting in her condo. It was the first meeting of three that were to determine if I was eligible for parenthood. It was another hoop, in a series of hoops, through which I had to jump. Attend a seminar on intercountry adoption. Get a criminal record check. Complete a prior contact check with BC's Ministry of Children and Family Development. Undergo a medical exmaination. Provide three personal references. Show my birth certificate. And my passport. Have an employer write a reference letter. Hand over financial statements. Marriage certificate, if applicable. Divorce decree, if applicable. And, of course, pay fees to the adoption agency, the Chinese Embassy, China Adoption Centre and an adoption service company whose services included visas, hotels, airfare, ground transport and guidance throughout the process when in China.

And to think, some people become parents with one drunken romp in the back of a Volkswagen.

But then, when women tell me tales of their horrific childbirth experiences, I can just say, "I bought mine."

I did not resent the homestudy C was conducting. Parenting should be a mandatory course in high school. One should definitely know why one wants to take on the most important job in the universe.

"I feel that besides working on every single *Ernest* movie, I have more to contribute to the world," I replied.

"How so?" asked C, her pen poised over paper.

"My mom has gifted me with a legacy that I now feel capable of passing on. Hard work ethic. Generosity. Moral compass. A pride in my culture."

Good answer, Patrice. Good answer.

"Do you speak Chinese?"

Uh oh.

"Unfortunately, my parents chose to speak Chinese only when they didn't want us to understand what they were saying. I'm second-generation Trinidadian. Trinidad was colonized by the Brits, so my mom was more of a stickler for the Queen's English."

"You've expressed interest in adopting from China?" C probed.

"Yes. The land of my ancestors and all that," I answered with a grin. "My great-grandparents hail from the villages of Toisan and Chungsan in the province of Guangdong."

"Have you thought about whether you'd like a boy or a girl, or does it matter?"

Well, that's a no-brainer. Girls are drowned in rivers, abandoned to die in fields, deemed unworthy of education, genitally mutilated and barely respected as caretakers and sperm receptacles the world over, is what I thought.

C's final report was to be instrumental in my application being approved by the British Columbia Ministry for Children and Families. Without their approval first, China would not even consider my application.

"I'd prefer a girl because I understand the challenges of being one," is what I said.

C continued, "And you're applying as a single parent?"

Okay, here we go. I was prepared for where this would lead. I had done my homework.

"Yes. My work is all consuming. Long hours. Travelling out of the country for months at a time. I've just never found the right partner."

That was true.

"How are you going to deal with the long hours as a single parent?" she asked.

Oh dear, she went off on a different tangent. Time to duck and weave.

"I've been fortunate to work for almost twenty years in a business that pays well, so I've got some money saved and I'm planning to stay home for a while. When I need to go back to work, I won't accept jobs out of the country. The novelty of living out of a suitcase has worn off anyway," I smiled sheepishly. Did that sound arrogant? I noticed C was making copious notes. I kept talking, trying to salvage the moment. "When I do eventually go back to work I'll hire a live-in caregiver. And my mom lives nearby and is willing to help." Outwardly, I appeared a capable, proud Asian woman; inwardly, I cringed. What would my dykes on the Drive have to say about me parading around my economic capabilities? Snap out of it, Patrice. There's an end game in play.

C finished writing and said, "As a single applicant you'll need to provide a letter from someone who is willing to be your child's guardian should something happen to you."

"Yes, I've already spoken to my older sister, Doi. She's also offered to accompany me to China when the time comes."

"That's lovely." C smiled and sized up my butch demeanour, which I'd tried to soften with the pearl earrings my mother had given me for my eighteenth birthday. "Also, the Canadian government doesn't care about this, but the Chinese government will require a notarized declaration that you're not a homosexual."

This was the moment for which I had prepared. I looked directly at C. Her salt and pepper hair was as short as mine.

"No problem," I said, without hesitation.

Oh, the wicked irony.

I tell my children not to lie. I tell them lying breaks trust. Damages relationships. And yet. And yet. I lied to get them.

In the early 2000s, the US was the country that took home the most children from China. Six thousand per year. Second place went to Spain, with six hundred per annum. The rumour was that the Christian evangelicals in the US donated a lot of money to Chinese orphanages to ensure most of those babies were going to good American Christian homes, a.k.a. nuclear families headed by heterosexual parents. When I went back for my second daughter in 2005, China was still allowing single, heterosexual parents to adopt, but the government had instituted a quota. Someone ahead of me in the quota line at my adoption agency happened to drop out, so I was able to adopt Tasia. *Whew!* Just a few months after touching down safely with Taje at the Vancouver International Airport, China ceased all single parent adoptions. Supposedly, the Chinese government had had enough of sneaky homosexuals posing as single hets in order to get Chinese children. Imagine that.

Yes, I lied. And I would do it again. Which, in fact, I did. I am as fucking worthy a parent as any white, heterosexual couple from Iowa. My children live in Vancouver, an Asian gateway. They have in me a role model that shatters the stereotype of the submissive little Asian girl. And some people even think my kids and I look alike. Well, white people do anyway.

As my sister and I sat with the twelve other adopting families in the departure lounge at the Vancouver International Airport, I wondered if anyone suspected I was one of those undercover homo parents, but no one seemed to care. There were two other single moms. Both white. One was accompanied by her sister and the other brought her mom. Everyone seemed bonded by, and more concerned with, the gravitas of our shared journey than with worry about so and so's sexual predilections. All of us were about to embark on a twelve-hour flight to Shanghai, followed by a four-hour layover and then a two-hour flight to Guangzhou in Guangdong. Add the time spent in airports and buses, and we would be travelling for more than twenty-four hours. It was to be the start of a two-week trip. One week was to be spent in Guangzhou waiting for our daughters' Chinese passports to be completed, and the other in Beijing, home of the Canadian Embassy, which would get their medicals and Canadian paperwork in order.

My sister was the perfect beard. She was the best foil for dampening the suspicions of the Chinese government. She is petite, feminine and straight. Like our mother, her makeup, hair, couture and accessories are always just so.

As for me, playing straight didn't prove too difficult as I stuck within the realm of my mien. I stayed away from skirts and dresses, as that would have raised the spectre of a bad drag queen. Instead I tried to copy the straight women I'd observed in Alberta farm country when I'd worked on a film in Rowley. Practicality with just a hint of the feminine. Petroleum jelly to gloss up the lips. Hair short, but not *too*. Comfortable shoes with a pizazz that went beyond the Birkenstock (thank you, New Balance). Cords with a wider wale. Mock turtlenecks so as not to draw attention to how handsome I looked in a button-up shirt. And of course, the pearl earrings my mother had hoped would keep the gay away.

The first test of my hetero-viability was when we went through customs in Shanghai. Truth be told, I wasn't nervous. I figured if they'd let me get this far (I'd had to send them a picture of myself with the application), I was probably in the clear. And I was right. The Chinese customs agent applied the usual stern scrutiny given to all foreigners and waved my sister and me through. Being part of an organized group that would help the Chinese government decrease the number of mouths it had to feed worked in my favour. Ordinary Chinese citizens had more important concerns than my sexuality. The wait staff in restaurants showed more disdain for my lack of a Chinese language than my lack of long hair. White people not being able to speak Chinese to their Chinese children they could somewhat accept. Me? Not so much. And whenever our group walked the streets with our new daughters, we were accosted by Chinese grandmothers who'd rush up and tug on our children's pant cuffs to cover any exposed skin. Their priority was clear: if you're going to take these precious girls from us please take care of them properly.

At 10:30 a.m. on January 6, 2003, my sister and I and the rest of our group found ourselves in a large, utilitarian room in the Guangdong Adoption Registration Office. Fatigue, anxiety and excitement filled the air. By the time our bus had pulled into the hotel the night before, it had been close to midnight. And now here we were, awaiting the arrival of our daughters. They too had been on a long journey of their own: the thirteen of them and their caregivers had endured a ten-hour bus ride from their orphanage in rural Guangdong. Us prospective families checked our watches and nervously chatted about nothing.

Suddenly, we heard some voices and a cacophony of what sounded like dog-toy squeaks. Then, accompanied by their caregivers, the first two little girls appeared, dressed identically in pink jackets, royal blue pants, yellow and blue striped shirts, and red shoes with squeaky noise-makers in their soles. As the two little girls were given to their new parents everyone started bawling, including the girls and their new parents. Two more little girls dressed in the same pink jackets, royal blue pants and red squeaky shoes were then brought in. And two more after that. Then finally, seventeen months after China had received my application to adopt, my little girl appeared in the arms of one of the caregivers. Just as I was headed toward them, the caregiver was pointed in my direction. Ceremoniously, we met halfway and the caregiver placed my daughter in my arms.

And so, we lived happily ever after. Right?

Always be careful what you wish for.

I had requested in my application a female infant between five and eight months. Keala was twenty-one months, which meant she had already been languishing in her orphanage for four months when my application arrived in China.

When I took Keala in my arms, she placed her hand ever so lightly on my shoulder and just stared at me. I smiled at her. Calling her by the name the orphanage had given her, I said, "Hello, Mei Xiao Jun. *Ni how ma?*" No reaction. My pronunciation might have been off-putting, but she didn't react much at all. She just continued to stare. Quizzically? Cautiously? Her shiny black eyes matched her shiny black hair. All around us babies were crying. Mei Xiao Jun-Keala? Not at all.

"Look, Trice," my sister said. "We got a good one. She's not a cry-cry."

I smiled and nodded in agreement. Little did I know. I should have wanted her to cry. Crying would have meant that in those critical first two years of her life she had bonded with someone. And when she was forced to leave them, her overwhelming grief would have manifested in a river of tears. Bonding creates pathways in the brain to empathy, the ability to read social cues, impulse control and feelings of security. Keala did not cry. And I, unfortunately, was ill-prepared and sorely unskilled to deal with the repercussions. Oh, sure, in one of the preparatory seminars I had heard something about reactive attachment disorder (RAD), but I had brushed it aside. I was going to be such a diligent parent that I'd be able to overcome anything.

Keala is not a movie set. I can't run her. There are no quick fixes for our relationship. My tiger-mother tactics exacerbate her anxieties, which in turn lead to behaviours that exacerbate my tiger-mother tactics. For years, we have mistaken each other's behaviours for truths. I see her obstinacy and argumentativeness as defiance instead of tools that help her survive anything from orphanages to mothers. My anger scares her. She is so terrified she can't see that my anger is borne of hurt at not being lovable enough to be listened to. With the support of many therapists and a host of lesbian aunties, we have only just begun to untangle this mess.

Our first few years together were so arduous I felt sorry for us both. I realized Keala needed more than me. She needed an ally. Hence, my decision to go back for number two: Tasia, previously known as Hong Yuan Fen.

My daughters require two different energies. While I am constantly applying the brakes with Keala, I am constantly pushing the gas pedal with Tasia. She is passive. When I brought her home from China she was thirteen months. Neither a crawler nor a walker, was she. Her muscle tone was so poor she couldn't even sit up by herself. I used to prop her head up and tip the bottle so the milk would drip into her mouth. She did not know how to suckle. Her developmental coordination disorder affects her academic, motor and social skills. She is less proficient than her peers by about three years, which affects her self-esteem and thus, her motivation. But her orphanage had been wise enough to find her a foster family, if only for a few months. The bonding pathways in her brain were pretty well formed. She knew how to cry.

When Tasia was placed in my arms it took her precisely nine minutes before she started howling. March 23, 2005. In another utilitarian room, in the Nanchang Adoption Registration Office, in the province of Jiangxi.

"I think this one's a cry-cry," my sister said loudly over Tasia's shrieks.

After a day and a half of vociferously expressing her distress, a hoarsened Tasia decided I wasn't going away and that I was her mama. Transference completed. From that moment on she was my little girl — much to my sister's chagrin. Henceforth during that trip, whenever I left Tasia in my sister's care, Taje, as we nicknamed her, would start sobbing to the point of hyperventilation.

"Hey, Madame Cry-Cry, your mother is just in the bathroom," my exasperated sister would say upon a Tasia outburst.

This motherhood thing. It's a forever journey, alright. My mother was eighty-eight when she died, and she parented up to her last breath. When my sister and I returned from China on both occasions and exited the sliding doors of International Arrivals with a new addition to the family, there stood my mother, handbag over her left arm, worriedly waiting to greet her newest grandchild.

She was so concerned about the welfare of my daughters and me that one Saturday while ironing she said to me, "Why don't you marry a rich, old man?" Never mind that in all my adult life I had never been dependent on a man, nor would I know what to do with one. However, this was proof that her thought processes had progressed to recognizing that if I didn't like men, I could at least marry one that would die soon and leave the three of us financially secure.

My mother embraced Keala and Tasia so profoundly that she exhibited a softness with them that had never before been bestowed upon her children or her first set of grandchildren. She invited my girls over to her house every Sunday, both to give me a break and to take them to church, so she could at least save their souls. When I went to pick them up on one of these Sundays, she handed me some containers of food and some advice. From her tone, I knew it wasn't aimed at a lesbian single mother, but rather to a comrade in parenthood.

"Don't make the same mistakes as me," she said.

Too late, Ma. Already did. Not even sure of all the ways I've messed them up yet. Keala is now sixteen, and Tasia thirteen. We continue our journey together, negotiating potholes every day. My contrarian Keala will always argue and question authority, but this will hold her in good stead in the age of Trumpian "truths." She's a fighter. Like me, she doesn't easily unpack emotions. They are uncomfortable places for us to dwell. But, she's smart enough to eventually learn. I know how hard it is. I struggle constantly to grow the nurturer part of my atavistic brain. Maybe one day we'll both get there.

My docile Tasia is in no hurry. Her stillness makes her receptive to emotions, to feelings. She is kind and cuddly. Gentle and full of empathy. We have a similar sense of humour. She has taught me there is joy to be had in motherhood. It does take her longer to learn things and that is frustrating for us both. Patience, as you have guessed, is not one of my natural virtues. We've had to develop strategies for everything from bouncing a ball to opening a jar to writing a school report. But because she is so likeable, people look out for her and help her. She will survive. By the grace of people like her grandmother.

Near the end of her life, my emaciated mother lay in her hospice bed succumbing to the ravages of cancer. And yet. And yet. She knew how to comfort my children: eight-year-old Keala would sit on one side of the bed, getting her back gently rubbed by her beloved Granny, whilst five-year-old Tasia sat on the other side of the bed, being allowed to just be. No words necessary.

As I remember these moments I realize that even if the jury's a long way from ruling on my parenting, I did three things right. My children did get to know my mother. She is indelibly and honourably etched in their memories. Secondly, my daughters have completely bonded with one another. They conspire, fight, love and have each other's backs. And lastly, when it came to choosing a name for my older daughter, I knew I wanted something imbued with the spirit of an island. The rhythms of the Caribbean are perfect for me. But my daughter would have her own rhythms. Perhaps somewhere in the Pacific. A link between China and Vancouver. Hawaii. Of course! I chose Keala. In Hawaiian, Keala means "pathway." And that she has been. And I am grateful.

INCONCEIVABLE

Caitlin Crawshaw

It's 6:26 p.m., and a very pregnant woman in a knee-length blue parka that no longer zips over her belly is standing at our front door. Her pale cheeks are pink from the cold, her blonde bob slightly askew from the wind. She is a few minutes early, as usual. I open the screen door and usher her into the house — it's too cold out there to linger.

"This is for *now*," she says, placing a plastic vial in my palm; it is warm to the touch and covered in heart stickers. Valentine's Day is a couple of days away. "And this," she places a Safeway bag into my other hand, "is for later."

I peek inside: blueberry bran muffins. They're so fresh that there's condensation on the inside of the Ziploc bag. "I figured you might be hungry after," she teases. But even if I'm not hungry, I will likely stress-eat the entire bag. The first time we tried to conceive, it was an open-hearted adventure and I was fearless; this time, I guard my heart, careful not to be too hopeful.

A big bear hug and then she's out the door, tromping through the snow in knee-high Sorels to the blue Mini Cooper where her husband is waiting. He waves from the driver's seat and I wave back. He's grinning from ear to ear. I'm not sure if it's because of his philanthropic gesture or because he's just had a happy ending.

After I take a couple of breaths, I speed walk to the bedroom where Jackie is sitting on the bed, waiting. She retrieves the needle-less syringe from the night table drawer. It's one of a half-dozen I purchased from a nearby pharmacy weeks earlier, mystifying the young pharmacist at the counter when I'd specifically asked for the kind *without* needles.

"Sick baby?" she'd asked.

"No, no baby yet."

"Then what do you need this for?"

Although I was the only person in line, I leaned in and whispered, "I'm doing an at-home insemination." I'd lingered a little too long on the "s" — like a lesbian snake. *Inssssssemination.*

Her brown eyes widened, but the rest of her round, pale face had maintained its professional demeanour — a real talent. "Oh ... okay. Well, these should work, then."

She handed me the 10cc needles, so I had to be more specific: "Just 5cc, please." The first time we tried the insemination, I'd been amazed at how little baby batter had been in the container — it fit perfectly into the smaller needle, which was the length of my ring finger. I'd had sex with men, but never had an opportunity, or reason, to really observe semen, let alone marvel at its hidden magic. The first time around, I stared at the donation with absolute wonder: the missing ingredient. Liquid gold, worthy of a moment of silence. The serum that would, incredibly, transform me into a mother. Despite the science — the basic, well-known, reproductive science — it seems inconceivable. Like creating something from nothing.

This time around, there's no ritual — no pause to take it all in. We get to business immediately, in an act that's more clinical than intimate. Afterward, I lie on the bed with a couple of pillows wedged under my hips and my legs up the wall. I'd read that it's generally advised to do this for at least ten minutes afterward, so I stick it out for a full thirty minutes before wandering out of the room, legs trembling.

"I feel like I just got off a horse," I tell Jackie.

I curl up with her on the couch and stare at the TV, watching, but not really watching. I'm wondering if a miracle has taken place inside of me — and whether the miracle will stick. And then I'm hoping the magic will work. And then I'm praying, silently. It's dangerous to think this way, but why wouldn't the stars align this time? Our journey thus far had been marked by serendipity. It was, after all, a chance encounter that led us to this point. And with a woman, no less.

Glancing around the conference room, my eyes fall on a pretty twenty-something sandwiched between a pair of middle-aged ladies. She wears her blond hair in a chin-length bob and looks both professional and fashion-forward in a khaki blazer, dark slacks and a blue blouse I'd admired at a clothing store a few weeks prior.

The woman focuses only on the presenter, occasionally scribbling some notes down on a pad of paper, smiling all the while. Her attention span is remarkable. Everyone else is occasionally whispering to one another and poking at their smart phones. I shouldn't stare like this, so I try to avert my eyes. Try and fail.

An hour later, we bump elbows in the snack room — while I am reaching for the bowl of candy — but I don't introduce myself. At the best of times, I'm a smidge awkward chatting with strangers and smiling on demand has never been a particular talent. And maybe as a side effect of schoolyard bullying, I tend to avoid good-looking people with social skills and gravitate instead to awkward underachievers. Naturally, I am fantastic at networking.

But a week later, at another conference in Edmonton, I'm waiting around to chat with a food writer after a marketing presentation when I notice the same woman standing behind me. Again, she is dressed demurely, and sports a confident smile and a black Coach handbag slung over her shoulder. I have one just like it. But I still don't make conversation, even though we're clearly the same age, have similar fashion sense and — apparently — enjoy conferences.

When it's my turn, I shake the limp hand of the author — a sixty-something-year-old woman with dyed blonde hair and the frown lines of a long-suffering newspaper journalist — and ask my question. I want to know how I should market myself if I choose to specialize in more than one type of thing: I am torn between essay writing, science journalism, visual art and some other stuff. I worry about how I'm supposed to brand myself — and these days, it's all about branding yourself.

"Get a business card and list the things you do on the back," she says, her pursed lips stretching into a short, stiff smile to signal the end of the transaction. She dismisses me by turning her back and mumbling "Good luck" over her shoulder.

"Awesome," I mutter under my breath.

"That was rude," whispers a voice behind me. "But you don't want marketing advice from someone who's published with eight different publishers."

I spin around, surprised by the solidarity. "Oh, I suppose so."

The woman extends her arm. "I'm Nancy," she says.

"I'm … Caitlin."

"Didn't I see you at the creative non-fiction conference in Banff last week?"

I feel my face flush. "Yeah, I think I saw you there, too."

"Wasn't it a great conference?"

"Sure was," I say, but when I try to substantiate the notion with details, my thoughts devolve into television static.

"Hey, there's some time before the next session. I was going to grab a coffee. Want to come with?"

We head to the refreshment table outside of the auditorium. Nancy tells me she's new in town; she moved a few months ago with her husband, an engineer working for an international company that moves its workers around a lot. Before this, they were in Wyoming, and before that Vancouver, finishing off master's degrees. Nancy writes about aviation and has just finished her first book.

"I sort of fell into it," she says. I can't stop imagining her in a brown leather aviator hat and a green flight suit, waving from the cockpit of an old-timey fixed-wing airplane. Like Amelia Earhart, the only female pilot I know of, although there must be more. "As you can imagine, there aren't many women who write about this," she says. Since I write about science, I can relate a bit.

We exchange business cards — miraculously, I find one that hasn't already been used as a Post-it note — and she asks if I'd like to grab coffee sometime. It's an easy sell. As it happens, I'm in the market for a new friend now that two dear friends and my little sister have relocated to other places. "Coffee would be great," I say.

A week later we meet at a coffee shop on the south side of town, halfway between my house and hers. She is already there when I arrive, this time dressed casually in a T-shirt and jeans, a pair of sunglasses perched on her head. Because I'm trying not to look like a total schlub, I spent some time picking out my outfit: jeans, a new blouse with a purple-and-blue pattern and copper-coloured open-toed flats. I even apply a bit of makeup. Friend dates are awkward for me: I want to look nice, like a person worth knowing, but not so nice that straight women wonder if I'm hitting on them. I'm terrified of being creepy.

She buys my coffee before I can stop her, which is tricky. "Oh, don't worry — I have a gift card from Christmas," she says, patting my forearm like a grandma. We sit down at a table on benches made of polished cross-sections of tree trunks. Everything in this joint is very organic looking. As I take my first sip of fair-trade coffee, I realize I'm already over-caffeinated and practically levitating off my chair.

We talk about the usual stuff, like pets. She and her husband have a cat and a dog, both rescues from Wyoming. I tell her about ours — two cats and a big galoot of a dog — also rescues. We also talk about where we're from: Nancy and her husband are from Ottawa. I am from boring old Edmonton. My partner is from small-town Alberta. I skirt around pronouns for as long as I can.

"What does he do?" she finally asks.

"He — I mean, *she* is a lab manager," I say, clearing my throat like a nervous old man. "She's a chemical technologist."

Nancy doesn't bat an eye. "Ah, so we both have science-y spouses! How long have you been together?"

"Six years," I say. "How about you guys?"

"Almost thirteen — we were high school sweethearts."

"Do you think you'll have kids?" I ask, forgetting that it's none of my business.

Nancy sighs. "Well, it's funny you ask that — my husband's finally worn me down and we're going to start trying soon. Or, at least, we're going to stop trying *not* to get pregnant."

I clap my hands together. "How exciting!"

"Well, I hope it takes a while. There's a lot I want to do with my career first."

"It's a hard balancing act."

"So, do you want to have a family?"

"Me?" I stammer. No one ever asks this. "Well, yeah. I do — I mean, we do. We came close a couple of months ago." I tell her of the gay friend-of-a-friend who cornered us at a birthday party to pitch his services as a sperm donor. He was twenty-one years old, but mature and well spoken. It helped that he was good looking, with features not so different from Jackie's and was positively thrilled by the prospect of helping lesbians start a family. We were dubious but charmed by his enthusiasm and figured we'd at least talk about it. Over the period of a couple of months we met at restaurants to discuss what we all wanted from the arrangement — courting him, in a way. When we were satisfied we wanted the same things — some contact, but no financial obligation or status as "daddy" — we decided to start trying. We asked him to do some blood work and, when it came back clear, felt confident about forgoing the invasive, time-consuming and expensive clinical route for a DIY approach. We'd all find a way to get over our collective awkwardness and do the insemination at home — no big deal. Then, the day before our first scheduled donation, he dumped us. His mother, apparently, had urged him to reconsider. She said he was too young to make such a life-altering decision. He didn't agree with her, but she was his mother, after all.

"That's horrible — I'm so sorry," Nancy says.

"It was probably for the best."

"I can't imagine," she says. "For us it's so easy. I mean, unless we have fertility problems, we'll just do the deed and make a baby."

Her sympathy is so genuine, so unexpected, that I start to panic. I chastise myself for oversharing with a perfect stranger;

why would she have any interest in my baby-making plans? I scan her face for micro-expressions — disgust? irritation? amusement? — but if she's making a mental note to delete my phone number, I can't tell. She frowns pensively.

"Well, why don't I ask my husband," she says, as if she's offering to lend out the bread maker.

"Oh — oh, no. *No, no, no.* You don't need to do that. *Really.* That's okay ... that's really kind, but I wasn't fishing. Honestly."

"No, I'm serious," she says, looking me dead in the eye. "It's not a big deal. Never hurts to ask." *Never hurts to ask? Who says that about sperm donation?*

"Are you sure?"

"Yeah, I'll talk to him. Hey — why don't you finish the last bit of my poppy seed bun?"

Within days of our coffee date, Nancy texts to say her husband was considering the idea. "But he wants to meet and talk about it," she adds. We plan to chat at their place instead of a restaurant, where nosy patrons might eavesdrop. After months of conversations with our first prospective donor, we'd grown tired of people leaning their chairs back to listen in.

On the night of our meeting, Jackie and I primp a little first. I wear jeans and a new blue blouse with a cardigan over top (it's early summer, but still chilly out). When we discover that we're both wearing the same shade of blue, Jackie puts on a green T-shirt: we don't want to look like matching lesbian salt-and-pepper shakers. Not tonight.

"I can't believe how fast this is happening," I say to Jackie in the car.

"Yeah, it's weird. I'm nervous," she says, leaning across the gearshift to take my hand. "But everything will be okay, you know, if it doesn't work out."

"I know," I say, but this is a lie. I've bitten my nails down to the quick and I feel sick to my stomach — I want a baby so badly it hurts. I tell myself over and over again to keep my expectations low. There are a million ways this could collapse, from cold feet and legal fears to co-dependent mothers. We could get close and he could pull out at the last minute, so to speak.

Somehow, I manage to compartmentalize on the drive over and focus on navigating the route. The Internet tells me that we only live ten minutes away from them, but even so I get confused and tell Jackie to take a few wrong turns. When we finally get there, we're late and I'm a ball of anxiety. My cheeks are warm and my ears are glowing red.

We pull up in front of a white bungalow in a quiet cul-de-sac in Millwoods. I undo my seatbelt like I'm a contestant in *The Amazing Race* ready to jump out of the car, sprint down the street, hop in a taxi, zoom down the highway to the airport and board a plane for Mexico. Jackie interrupts my thoughts by grabbing my arm and leaning in for a kiss. I'm suddenly aware of my dry lips and realize, in horror, that I've forgotten my lip balm at home. I never leave home without it.

Jackie carries in a six-pack of beer; I carry in a greasy brown bag filled with samosas from the Indian place nearby. I can't help but feel like we're all on a date, but there's even more at stake — and many more opportunities for awkwardness. At some point, when we've talked about the life-changing ramifications of making a baby and whether we want to be tethered together for the rest of our lives, we will talk about practical issues. Like, how will we arrange for the donation? Will we pick it up from them, or will they deliver it? How big a cup will he need? Will the idea of two lesbians sitting in a living room awaiting his donation be a total boner killer? Oh god ... I am thinking about boners. *We should call this off,* I think. *I'm too pervy to breed.*

We're hardly at the door when a large dog starts barking inside. As the storm door opens, I see Nancy dragging a one-hundred-pound beast away by his collar: "Down! Lie down, Riker!" The dog whines as he collapses in his bed, ears back and tail wagging frantically. Her husband laughs sheepishly as he greets us at the door; his teeth are straight and white, like little picket fences. I tell him not to worry — our dog is a drama queen, too. And not nearly as well trained.

Like Nancy, Elliott is blonde and blue-eyed with light skin, about as Caucasian as a person can be. His hair has begun to recede, so it is cut close to the scalp. With a strong chin, smooth skin and a hint of dimples on both cheeks, he's universally handsome. He's also tall — about six feet, from what I can tell – and has an athletic build that fills out his T-shirt. We've already met once before — he and Nancy came to my art show a few weeks after our fateful coffee date — but he looks different this time. His smile seems warmer, his voice gentler. Maybe it's because he's not just my new friend's husband: now he's the manly saint who will make us a family. Well, maybe.

"Come on in," he says, gesturing with one arm. We step in and slip off our shoes. Glancing around I see that the layout of their mid-seventies home is a lot like our own mid-sixties home: at the end of a narrow living room there's a fireplace and a small dining room around the corner. The place is clutter-free and decorated in hues of taupe, beige and light blue. Our taste in décor is weirdly similar.

I set the samosas down on the dining room table, next to the chips and guacamole Nancy has already laid out; Jackie brings the beer to the kitchen, like we've been there a million times.

"Kronenberg," says Elliott, turning a bottle over in his hands. "A good yuppie beer."

"You passed the first test," Nancy jokes. "We love beer — especially this guy. And the samosas smell amazing."

We settle into the living room couches and chit-chat about our careers, hobbies, houses — first date stuff, more or less. I zone in and out of the conversation, preoccupied by the striped pattern on the ottoman, which matches the cushions, and the fluffy black cat that strolls in and out of the room, flicking his tail like our cat does. I stare at the pictures on the walls, the vertical blinds, the laminate wood floor, the occasional tumbleweed of cat hair hiding under a chair. All of this feels comfortable and even familiar —

like we already know them. Like they're a heterosexual version of us.

Once we've eaten the greasy food and polished off most of the beer, Nancy finds a creative segue into the topic of baby making and I return to my body, anchored to reality by my raging anxiety. Try as I may, I can't stop my hands from shaking or my gut from roiling. I'm waiting for him to tell us that it's a terrible idea, that he said yes on a whim or to please his wife. Or maybe Nancy's turned off by the idea of her husband being the biological father of some other woman's child. Or maybe they'll both tell us that it was actually an elaborate ruse, that they're actually Baptists looking to convert us and pray away the gay.

"I think we're in," Elliott says carefully, "but we need to talk about everyone's expectations. We want to make sure that we all know what we're getting ourselves into."

Nancy nods. "We love the idea of helping a gay couple start a family. We feel really privileged that, as a straight couple, we can make a baby so easily."

"But we need to make sure we aren't going to be responsible for supporting this baby in any way," Elliott adds. "That's the biggest thing I worry about."

Jackie and I have already thought this through. We decided we would hire a lawyer to draft an agreement and, if they wanted representation separately, we would pay for that, too. We would make sure that under no circumstances would they pay out of pocket for any part of the process.

We talk through other things, too, like whether they'll be in our baby's life. It's something we really want. Otherwise, we would've gone to the fertility clinic in town for the sake of anonymity, like most lesbians do.

"We want a donor who'd be like ... an uncle," I say. "And we want everything to be in the open, so our child knows where they came from." I meet Jackie's eyes to make sure I'm wording this well. In this situation, I am our unofficial ambassador, and I worry I'm bungling this up. But Jackie meets my eye and nods in agreement.

To most people, this uncle-daddy concept is a bit boggling, but they are unfazed. "That would work for us," says Nancy. I wonder if they've thought through some of the logistics of this ahead of time. Maybe even read up on queer families. Nothing we're talking about seems new to them.

After this, we go downstairs to look at family photos, smiling faces of strangers in framed photos on a fireplace mantle in the rec room. Elliott has a stepfather and a younger brother in Ontario, but his mother and father have passed away. It breaks my heart to hear it — he's so young to have lost both parents — but I feel my shoulders relax. There's no mother to talk him out of it.

We look at their wedding photos and pictures of Nancy — an only child — with her parents, who live outside of Ottawa. Her family is beautiful, too. Then we sit down around the coffee table where they've laid out a photo album for us.

"Would you like to see baby pictures?" Nancy asks.

"Sorry, it's kind of dorky. We thought you might be curious," says Elliott.

But of course we want to see them; if he's going to be the biological father of our child, this is a sneak-peek of what's to come. Theoretically, our child should look something like the chubby, blue-eyed baby staring back at us from the yellowing pages of the album.

Elliott slowly narrates as we go through it. There are the baby-eating-food-for-the-first-time photos, silly toddler pictures, posed vacation shots — the usual stuff. It looks like Elliott had a happy childhood, even though he lost his father before he was a teenager.

Eventually we have to disband. We exchange hugs at the door and Jackie and I drive home, dizzy with possibilities.

"Is this really going to happen?" asks Jackie, point blank.

"I hope so," I say. But I've probably jinxed us.

A few months later we all have dinner at a hole-in-the-wall Caribbean restaurant. The place is tiny, with a grey-tile floor, orange walls and black wooden chairs and tables. It smells like fried chicken and curry. It's not our first choice of restaurant: spicy food triggers my IBS and Jackie only likes Asian-fusion. But Nancy has a Groupon.

This is one of a dozen double dates we've been on in the last few months. Like usual, conversation moves freely and is punctuated by Nancy's inappropriate jokes and Jackie's work stories. Elliott and I are typically quieter, jumping into the conversation only occasionally.

After our drinks arrive — three Red Stripes and a ginger beer — we get the news: Nancy is pregnant. The baby is due in May. They're both smiling wide, holding hands under the table. I stand up first, scraping my chair against the tile floor, shrieking, "Oh my god!" We all exchange hugs.

"First try," says Nancy, glancing at Elliott. He is smiling shyly, but proudly. "Turns out Elliott's not shooting blanks, which is good news for you guys!"

"Well, you didn't really think that I'd be —"

"— Nah, I'm just teasing," Nancy says, and gives him a kiss on the cheek.

A month later, we start Operation Gayby. I hit up the Costco pharmacy and buy a bulk pack of pregnancy tests and an ovulation predictor kit. I'm convinced it'll take us dozens of attempts or never work at all. Naturally, because of our luck in finally finding a donor who (probably) won't back out, the next part of the process should fail miserably.

But like Nancy, I get pregnant on the first try. Over pasta, we giggle about how fun it will be to be pregnant together and how close in age our children will be. "We'll be like sister wives," she laughs. She emails me names and contact details for local midwives, since it's virtually impossible to get one after five weeks of pregnancy. We talk about maternity fashion and what our writing lives will look like after our babies arrive. We wonder what kind of grandmothers our mothers will be. And then, I miscarry.

We wait a few months to try again. By then, Nancy is in her third trimester and long past the magic of it all. She's spent months on modified bed rest thanks to a rare pregnancy complication that made her susceptible to preterm labour. She is now utterly finished with this pregnancy bullshit. Even so, she is unfazed by our request for more donations. She throws on her parka and boots and makes the trek to our house in the goddamn winter. Elliott waves from the driver's seat of their car as Nancy — ever the rugged Canadian — stomps through the snow to the front door, eager to make the delivery. As she waddles back to the car, I have a thought: unless she needs an organ one day, I will never be able to repay her kindness. Nor Elliott's, of course. Whether we make a baby or not, this is the best gift I've ever received, by a (frozen Canadian) mile.

Months later, I stumble out of bed to the bathroom at 7 a.m. desperate to pee. But before I do, I suddenly remember to grab a pregnancy test from the cabinet and tear open the plastic. I pee on the stick — as I've done so many times before — set it on the edge of the sink. Wait thirty seconds.

A faint, blue line appears in a circle. Squint a little. Maybe it's two lines? It's definitely two lines.

I check the back of the pregnancy kit to confirm. One line and I'm still just me. A second line: Something is growing inside of me.

I'm suddenly aware that my face feels stiff — like it's stuck somewhere between an ear-to-ear smile and a grimace, as if I'm about to tell a lie. I crawl into bed, spoon Jackie and whisper, "I'm pregnant." It can't be real — but it's true. I really am pregnant again. She mumbles something but doesn't wake.

I'm twitchy, so I get out of bed again and pee on three more pregnancy tests. "You're *pregnant*!" I whisper to myself. "Pregnant, pregnant, pregnant!" I scrutinize myself in the mirror, pulling up my tee shirt to check out my naked belly. But I look exactly like I did yesterday — minus the insuppressible smile that's taken over my face. Then I do a little happy dance (quietly), hop into bed again and stare at Jackie's back, willing her to finally wake up.

Darkness and Beauty: The Making of Lesbian Moms

Emily Cummins-Woods

I wish I could say it happened one full-moon evening, the candle-light creating suggestive shadows on the wall as our bodies moved together, building in rhythm. That this sexy woman I married brought me to the edge of ecstasy, inserting the magical ingredient just as I crested over the edge and I took in our combined love, hopes and dreams. That nine months later, a healthy baby would effortlessly appear. My perfect, lesbian conception fantasy, once upon a time. The truth is much more awkward, a whirlwind of a dance.

Alice and I met over eighteen years ago in a university class on Eastern religions. We were so young! She and I, still so naïve about real grown-up life, had serious doe eyes for each other. Things really began for us after a New Moon women's circle when Alice bravely asked me out. Within days after our first date, where she wore those wild red pants and we shivered through first kisses in the trees, we had already checked with each other that each of us wanted kids. That was kind of odd for twenty-three-year-olds in our world in the late nineties.

Fast forward several years: we travelled together, did organic farming in Europe and PEI, and then settled into our first apartment together in Montreal with a couple of cats (lesbians, remember?). I gently nudged Alice into proposing to me (she did a sweet job!) and we had a magical, community-oriented wedding soon after it was legal to do so. We felt we had made a nice box to put kids into and decided it was time to start Project Family. First, we needed a name. We thought our combined last names would be too long and that picking one of them would be unfair. Lying in the forest on a blanket, looking up at the tall trees, we decided on being the Woods family. We both had the name Wood in our recent ancestry. When we combined them, turning it into the plural Woods, we made the name alive.

Then there was the sperm thing. Being geeks, we researched and *researched* the options in Quebec at the time. The law had evolved, thankfully, to the point where as long as we didn't get preggers by actually sleeping with any bio-guys, our babies would be ours alone. We made a list of potential studs, including a former gay roommate, whose rejection of our invitation made me sad for years. We asked a handful of other men, getting more frustrated each time. Jack off in a cup, sign here; how hard could it be? Finally, a totally wonderful guy we knew said yes. He had his blood and sperm tested, and we wrote up a contract and signed it, knowing it wasn't legally binding but would at least express our mutual intent. No responsibilities toward each other, no co-parenting, no demands. Alice and I both agreed I would try first, since I really wanted to get pregnant. We got seriously fertility savvy by charting my periods and checking my cervical mucus (stretchy ... it's time!).

When we finally tried conceiving in 2007, we *did* light candles and attempt a romantic frame of mind, similar to that initial fantasy. We were giggling as Alice filled the syringe with semen. It's so gooey at first, liquefying eventually, and what a unique smell! I didn't know! We were so careful to get every drop of our liquid gold. There were some kisses between us, but we were mostly anxious to get my legs up the wall. I had every expectation that we would hit a home run. I thought my egg would get out its biggest catcher's mitts when it saw those sperm swimming forward for the first time! I floated through those next two weeks, graciously loving every jerk driver and rude client. Alice and I were generous with one another too, taking a belated honeymoon to Glastonbury, snuggling in the mornings and making plans for our family life. I was totally, and I mean totally, unprepared for that first one-line preggie stick followed by a period. The book of rules for the world as I knew it felt like it had burned to ashes. My female parts had betrayed me.

We rallied and tried again, and then again. The romantic flavour of the project was ebbing by then. Our donor moved to the US and we still drove the seven hours down when I happened to be ovulating on weekends. I went to reiki, counselling and osteopathy appointments, and did meditation and yoga daily. I visualized the heck out of all of it, imagining funny scenarios like the egg being this sweet gay surfer and the sperm an arriving gang of bikers with a burly stud in the lead. I enjoyed those playful images, but often my visualizations were more about finding my shadows and trying to shed light into broken places; finding closed doors and opening them wide. Despite these efforts, every cycle felt like the proverbial person who keeps walking into the same hole despite knowing it's there. Eventually, exhausted by the travel and timing challenges, we decided to stop using that donor (whom we still love).

Next, we decided to try the clinic route. Good lord. Our whole life and bodies were laid bare. Since lesbians are considered "functionally infertile," we could at least use the hospital service in Ontario, which provided free fertility testing and insemination. Ironically, we sat in the same waiting room as the women getting abortions. After an intimate physical, and many questions, we then had to be cleared by a psychiatrist. The reward for passing a psych test, besides the dubious distinction of being considered sane enough to become parents? A hysterosalpingogram (HSG). If you've never had an HSG, I wouldn't wish it on you even if you are a truly wicked person and/or get pregnant really easily. A special tiny speculum is inserted into the cervix; fluid is then shot up and into each fallopian tube to make sure it's clear. I barely got through them checking one tube before demanding an end to the excruciating procedure. At least we were cleared to begin inseminating.

Looking at those catalogues was like being in an anthropological experiment. Who will the white middle-class lesbos choose? Mr. Perfect must be intelligent, kind and ideally have physical features similar to Alice's. We also thought we'd go for guys who wrote nice letters to their future spawn. We wanted them to be mentally and physically healthy, with careers and with what seemed like a decent head on their shoulders. We opted for a European company based in Copenhagen, since they only allow ten families to be created per donor, unlike the American sperm banks, which allow thirty-five each. We fantasized about going to Denmark with our children, introducing them to the "happiest people on earth" and meeting their donor Titus or maybe Sven when they turned eighteen. Did I mention it costs more for the right to contact the donors when our kids reach legal age? The sperm, you see, was not free. Plus, we were recommended to use two vials per cycle, which totalled fourteen hundred dollars per month! We got a line of credit.

Despite the cost, and with renewed enthusiasm, we bravely jumped into this new stage of our family-making. The no-nonsense nurse made us sign a form to confirm that the correct donor number was on the vial. Was it right? We couldn't remember, but it seemed right (oh god!). We held hands as the nurse filled a long, straw-like catheter with the special juice and warned me the intrauterine insemination (IUI) would be uncomfortable, and that my body would rebel, contract and maybe bleed that day. She was right. I still cross my legs and cringe remembering the sensations.

Then we waited. Today, when we've had a particularly long day of parenting, I try and remember how much waiting and wanting went into all this. We put our bodies, souls and our relationship on the line for a wish of the heart. A wish that got harder to grasp as the whys and wherefores became more mysterious. The last two weeks of every insemination cycle became more emotionally painful. I hit a very dark place where nothing felt possible; where my faith in myself and in life waivered.

I knew that if I went through twelve cycles of insemination without pregnancy I would be considered infertile. I refused to accept that title. It had been several months since we had upped my medical interventions: we added ultrasounds and blood tests, and Alice had been giving me Ovidrel shots to induce ovulation. Shortly before my twelfth insemination, after my transvaginal ultrasound, I received that cycle's second prick of the needle. It would be my last visit to that clinic. Something snapped in me and I began to cry old, sad tears. I explained to the nurse that I was done and left on shaky legs. By that point it was a relief.

We still had sperm on ice, though. We quickly switched gears: Alice whipped through the fertility obstacle course, had the dreaded HSG (a bond we will always share) and off we went to her first insemination. (It was awful.) Nothing. Another try; still nothing. She was supposed to be the fertile one! My parents took years to make me, and my conception involved secret fertility rituals on Saint Kitts while my parents studied monkeys and god knows what else. Alice's mom, on the other hand, just had to look at her dad to get pregnant. There were also the financial stresses: each cycle was driving us deeper into debt, not to mention the junk food and therapy bills! We were officially broke. We were set to hang up the towel and contact adoption agencies when something miraculous happened. We still can't believe it.

One night, a very good friend of ours was eating a meal with a married couple, a man and woman, who didn't have children. She asked them whether they planned on having kids; the man replied that they didn't want any themselves, but if they knew a nice lesbian couple ... They were serious. So, we met. Blood and sperm tests were done. A contract was written very similar to the one with our first known donor. When we were all ready, I went to pick up a warm cup wrapped in a white gym sock, which I stuffed down my shirt and drove home like a bat out of hell. Alice waited for me at home in the "position," which meant she should've had her pelvis on a pillow while thinking positively, but she was possibly reading a murder mystery instead. I ran upstairs and filled that 3cc syringe while she muttered nervous instructions at me. Then I sent a million or so potential hitters off to find that egg! And folks, I am happy to report that those savvy little navigators did just that. About six weeks after that fortuitous dinner, and soon after an awesome road trip to New Orleans together, Benjamin was conceived.

Alice became totally, horribly nauseous *all the time*. Mornings my tush. She had life sickness! Soon she started popping Diclectin (the miracle pill) and was asking for Pop Tarts and granola with yogurt at all hours. Despite the pills, she felt sick for nine long months. I know she had it hard, but it was also really challenging for me to lie next to her in bed and rub salve onto her bulging belly; I wished it was me and I wondered about fate, feeling it was all so unfair. Sometimes I cried quietly in bed, her bump touching my back. I read our little peanut stories through the womb to bond with him, especially one about a little boy with two moms and a mouse friend named Alice. He loved that book as a baby!

The day he was born — three weeks before the due date — our home was having an intense bathroom renovation done. We went for Alice's check-up at the midwives' office. Alice thought she'd been peeing her pants that day, weirdly often and a lot, so they tested her and found amniotic fluid. She was in labour! We hurried home, ran a bath and made calls. She hated the bath, so we made up the bed with plastic sheets under the regular cotton ones. Friends arrived, and eventually Alice's mother and sister joined them, too. Our contractor asked if he should leave and Alice bellowed, "NO! Get that bathroom done!" So, he hummed and sang as he worked his way through Alice's awesome, animalistic moaning and grunting and powerfully fast labour. I'll never forget the look in her eyes, that totally feral fear. Within a few hours, and after a long time pushing, our first child was born. The pain was washed away in a flood of the warmest love.

And wow, did he look like our donor, Steve. I mean, it was uncanny. His skin was a golden tan (after it stopped being purple), his dark hair and dark eyes contrasting against Alice's pale arms and chest. Our baby boy looked thoughtful from the very beginning. The cats and I curled up protectively around the two of them, proud and tired and happy. We nested that way, more or less, for three days. Then, instead of tan like Steve or pale like Alice, our baby turned yellow.

The neonatal intensive care unit (NICU) phase in our new little family's life is one we would prefer to forget. We had just figured out his name was Benjamin when he was whisked to the hospital with severe jaundice. The tiny creature was poked and prodded for blood samples, Alice couldn't nurse him for a few days and he was in isolation (being a "dirty baby" born at home). He was hooked up to machines and placed under special lights. This was a dark time, for Alice especially. She couldn't hold this new baby, whom she had kept safe within her all that time. Her body had been blown open and her milk was coming up, too. I had to fight for the nurses to feed Ben breast milk and finally, with the help of the midwives, for Alice to nurse him directly. We slept at the hospital in a fancy wing just for parents of serious NICU cases. They nearly had to put in a central IV line through Ben's belly button and completely replace his blood. He fought off the jaundice a few days later, and we got to take care of him ourselves in our own room. Eventually, we could head home and begin our life together.

The year that followed was a further shock to our systems, both existentially and practically. Ben needed a lot of holding and rocking and he was not a good sleeper. Alice had post-partum depression and I had some other kind of "what happened to my life/wife?" syndrome. We were a wreck. We loved our beautiful, miraculous baby with the deep eyes of an old soul, and yet we were struggling to figure out this mommy-bliss we saw in other parents. Alice opened her heart to the world and all its suffering and her fear and anxiety for Ben were intense. I felt more tired than I thought possible, and though I did a good chunk of the baby care, I still felt left out. My dark self, usually so well suppressed, demanded exposure. I began to express a selfish, angry, possessive side of myself. I'm also a ginger, and we are well known for our tempers. As it turns out, super tired, jealous, neglected gingers get volcanic.

There were many highs, though. I relished playing with Ben and watching him acquire language. I was speaking to him in French back then; my name is Maman. (Alice, being a Brit, is Mummy.) He had the cutest expressions for things and could be such a ham, shaking his booty and singing! We had a lot of fun running around, wrestling and building endless forts. We also had play dates with Doni Steve every month or so (he'd acquired a title by then), and sometimes his wife came, too. I was hesitant at first about where he fit into the mix; whether I'd feel territorial. That all evaporated as he became the beloved "cool guy" we knew; he was super fun, had musical and carpentry skills and a big van. He loved our son, too, and was utterly unobtrusive in our raising of him.

We explained to Ben from day one that it took many ingredients to make him, like the muffins we made together on those bleary-eyed mornings. Into the uterus bowl went an egg from Mummy, a sperm from Doni Steve and lots of love from Maman. To this day he remains unfazed by any of those details. A kid in kindergarten once told him having two mothers was stupid, and he waited a long time to tell us. We helped him come up with responses for the future and it's been fine. We're lucky to know several families with two moms, so it's just normal. Honestly, Ben has spent more time processing being vegetarian. Anyway, the toddler years were busy and funny and are mostly blurry now (thank goodness for cameras). During that era, every few weeks Alice would suggest it was time for me to try again for a sibling for this rowdy little monkey.

I'm not sure what made me ready to try again. We're both glad we decided ahead of time about having two kids (minimum). It's easy to see why people stop at one, but we were committed and reconnecting more now that Ben was bigger. It was time. I bravely pushed that creaky, tightly sealed door open once again.

My first try is fuzzy (we all got sick that month), but the second try I remember well. Despite the planet Venus being large in the night sky, we were pretty grumpy with each other. Steve's parents were coming to town so he could only give us one sample that cycle, too. Alice emptied the full syringe near my cervix and left me to go deal with our toddler, the laundry or whatever else. I didn't visualize anything, didn't do any yoga poses. I genuinely believed it to be impossible for it to work this time, or maybe ever. So much for the power of positivity!

I know lesbians cannot have babies by accident. There are no surprises we didn't work our butts off to achieve. Nonetheless, I can honestly say that I was shocked into disbelief when I peed on a stick and saw two lines. I did the test alone, unlike all the other times in the past when we eagerly awaited results together. Alice was on the floor with Ben in his room and it was painfully early in the morning. I walked in with a funny look on my face and said, "Hey guys, you'll never guess!" They didn't. "I'm pregnant!"

How on earth did it finally happen for me? Was it Venus? Was it going vegan for six months prior? Maybe having a baby in the house already helped the hormone soup. After Ben's birth, I had an important attitude shift from pregnancy being about me, my spiritual journey and my failing body to it being about wanting to increase our family. I saw my pregnancy now as the conduit for more joy. What also helped, and likely most potently, was that our donor has super-sperm. Seriously, what a stud. The first time we tried with him, Alice conceived Ben. The second try worked for me. Lastly, there is of course the ephemeral, ineffable quality of mystery, and our infuriating utter lack of control over the creation of life.

Unlike poor Alice, I had a fun and easy pregnancy. I painted my naked body, had a belly blessing and generally walked around like an Earth Mama. I had no weird physical issues except low iron. Since we were parents already, life just carried on. Alice said she was glad I was good at self-care because she had her hands full. Almost exactly right on my due date, my contractions began. I had created a beautiful womb-like room in our house to give birth in, with an inflated tub full of warm water, posters with beautiful sayings and pictures hanging all over, and a mix tape of chanting and other songs. Good friends took Ben, others stayed with me (some even into the tub to press down on my back) and my mom held my hands. It was a cosmic trip; I charged into the pain of each contraction on my imaginary black stallion, shooting targets into the trees like Merida in *Brave*. Apart from the many unpleasant attempts to get a line for antibiotics into the dehydrated veins of my hand (even my friend, a veterinarian, tried), it was a dream labour. But when my waters finally broke, in a wonderful rushing feeling, the midwives found baby poop in 'em! Meconium is dangerous for babies, so they gently explained we'd have to go to the hospital (a big fear of mine), which I first resisted, and then had to accept. During the ambulance ride, I chanted loudly to drown out the sirens and kept my eyes closed until we were in the birthing room.

Daniel's actual birth was scary. I was completely exhausted from pushing and was beginning to feel defeated. Daniel needed vacuum suctioning to be born, so there was a transfer of care to the doctors. Our original fertility doctor came and showed me a pair of scissors. He said, "The baby comes out on the next push or —" *Snip, snip.* That hateful act was motivating! Daniel finally emerged, and I tore soon after. He was so quiet and needed intubation. It felt like an eternity, but soon his voice echoed around me and he was in my arms.

He and I lived together in the children's wards for three more days, taking each other in. I had my thirty-sixth birthday there and received a special birthday lunch from the kitchen, complete with stickers and a cupcake. The reason for our stay, however, was that our baby refused to pee. For the second time in our life, our new tiny boy had to have so many medical interventions. At least Daniel, whose name took us even longer to choose, could mostly stay with me. Once they started talking about surgery in Ottawa, I called a reiki master I knew. Whether you believe in reiki or not — and I do — he peed while she was giving him a treatment by distance, turning the strip on his special diaper a long-awaited green. The doctors couldn't believe it. We were soon cleared to go home.

My early days with Daniel were dreamy. I loved being at home with him, going on adventures, grinning at each other. He was a cheery little guy, quick to walk and eager to catch up with his hero Ben. His personality was different than his brother's: less thought and more action, and a lot more boo-boos! He still loves Band-Aids.

He was more outgoing and had more interest in cooing at grannies in grocery lines. Daniel has a fierier temper, too, being of old Scottish blood. They both have second-generation Italian and Russian genes from Steve, but Daniel was generally easy, loved to sleep and loved squishing our cats. Benjamin was protective of him and sometimes jealous, especially when Daniel began to grab things. In general, though, we avoided some of the more typical jealousy issues by each boy having his own bio-mom.

Our family felt complete. Our relationship as mothers felt more equal, too: now we both had the experience of being bio-moms and non-bio moms, and we had deep empathy for the highs and lows inherent in each role. The truth is, the roles don't feel the same; the love is just as deep for each child, as is the desire to protect them, but Alice and I learned of the unique bond that comes from carrying a child inside our wombs. It was intense at first, and then it waned over the years to even out between both our children. The boys point out who carried them and sometimes in their simple way equate that with more love. They never say one of us isn't their mother. We are so glad they each have a sibling, despite the squabbles. They build forts together now, roam the woods and snuggle with flashlights in their closet. Their Lego creations are so imaginative. We all love a good potty joke, have family dance parties, go camping, eat a lot, scooter everywhere and dream of driving an RV around together. We celebrate each and every milestone of their growing up (and ours, really).

It isn't perfect. Alice and I are regularly sent to the edge of our limits, buttons are pushed on all sides and the kids lose their minds and explode with "big feelings." Heaven knows we moms have our share of those, too! But we're a family; we're the Woods family. We made us who we are. We are not defined by some prescribed idea of family; rather, we reinvent the lived experience of that word every day, as we add Donis, a third set of grandparents and close friends to the mix. None of us would change it for the world.

WHAT IF YOUR KIDS GROW UP TO BE STRAIGHT?

Jane Byers

A few days into our fourteen-day parenting trial-by-fire, we suggested taking the twin toddlers that we were in the process of adopting for a hike. The foster mom, who regarded nature as something to be feared and avoided, suggested a walk at the mall instead, remarking that they'd never been outside in winter. We had to get away from the TV and small quarters and desperately wanted time with the twins alone, not to mention the fresh air we craved and had become accustomed to with our outdoor lifestyle. We gave the foster mom a day to get used to the idea and went the following morning, which was sunny and mild for February. We walked around their acreage on a bench overlooking a lake and down the adjacent country road with the twins on our backs. They looked like deer caught in headlights. Our son soon grew to love it, though, and wanted to go in the backpack again. Our daughter, typically the more skeptical one early on, wasn't so sure. The foster mother gasped with relief when we returned from that first hike. I don't think hiking was quite what she meant, however, when she asked us how we felt about going to hell for our "lifestyle." This was definitely the low point in our two weeks. After taking a deep breath and concealing my incredulity, I suggested we just focus on the kids and told her we didn't think it would be helpful to get into her beliefs.

The twins lived with foster parents for the first fourteen months of their lives. We were being considered as prospective adoptive parents to this boy and girl, along with about eight other couples initially. Every two weeks or so we got an update from the social worker, stating that we were still "in," as they whittled it down to six families, then four, and so on … We were particularly nervous about this process after being told we were not a model family for many social workers, since we were a same-sex couple. We were asked to do a number of things that we considered extra work because of our same-sex family status — a gay tax, we jokingly called it. Nevertheless, we overachieved when asked to write an essay on how we would provide the twins, especially the boy, with positive male role models. We hastily made calls to our male friends confirming weekly play dates and mentorship opportunities. When asked how we will provide opportunities for exposure to their ethnic heritage, given that their bio-mom was originally from Southern India, we laid out plans in thoughtful detail. We planned to visit large metropolitan areas every chance we had, attend Diwali and eat Indian feasts weekly. Eventually, we were told it was down to us and another family. Being competitive in team sports, we referred to this as the finals, sudden death.

So it came to be, after many months, that we sat in a government boardroom, with beige walls and a view of the Kelowna sprawl, and met with the evangelical Christian foster parents of the twins. She: soft-featured, maternal and smiling; he: thin, angular and slightly combative, both with thick Scottish accents. They sat at one end of the large table and we at the other, buffered by three social workers. The foster parents' accents put me at some ease. Perhaps I was endeared to the Scots as a Northern England native; I earned the family right to don a tartan after my people fought with the Scottish against the English in the Border Wars. Fundamentalism wrapped in a Scottish accent was more palatable somehow. Or perhaps it was my inclination, when face to face, to find the common ground, knowing that whatever topical differences there are, we humans share many more commonalities.

Normally this meeting would not take place. Normally we would meet the kids at the same time as the foster parents and start the adoption transition. However, we were meeting so the

Christians could get to know us and ask some questions, noting that they had never knowingly talked to any "homosexuals," according to the social worker.

At the time I couldn't have clearly articulated it, but the foster parents considered our "behaviour" an illness, while we considered it our identity. We were meeting to give them an opportunity to accept, or at least tolerate, us before we landed on their doorstep every day for two weeks while we got to know the children's routines by being with them for every waking hour. Little did we know, but we were meeting so the social workers had an alternative to yanking the children out of their home if the foster parents refused to cooperate with and sanction us as the new parents. Sanctioning is a big part of why we had the overlap, so the kids, not yet verbal, could see the foster parents giving us permission to parent; as we fed them and bathed them while the foster parents were present, the kids would come to think of us as safe and familiar and eventually bond. Over those fourteen days, they came to follow us around like ducklings imprinting on what was near.

It was the most important job interview of our lives. One of their questions during that meeting was, "What will you do if your children grow up to be straight?" While we would later laugh and shake our heads at the absurdity of this, the foster parents were just expressing what many privately fear. That we can make our children decide their sexuality is a naïve though pervasive belief; it is the impetus for insisting boys wear blue clothes, not pink, for refusing boys the freedom to play with dolls or to cry, and for encouraging passive activities instead of aggressive ones, such as contact sports, for girls.

I always think of the brilliant line in the nineties movie *Leaving Normal* when Darly, played by Christine Lahti, says of a kid's room, adorned with hockey and aviation memorabilia and in which she is bunking for the night: "Oh my god. This room has 'Please God, don't make my son a fag' written all over it."

This reflects, at best, a misunderstanding about vertical and horizontal identity. Andrew Solomon, in his book, *Far from the*

Tree: Parents, Children, and the Search for Identity, defines vertical identities as those that are passed down generationally from parent to child, like language, ethnicity and sometimes religion. We don't try to cure vertical identity within families for it is not seen as an issue. Horizontal identities, on the other hand, are not passed down. They have often been thought of as illnesses, e.g., deafness, dwarfism and queerness. These identities are alien from the parents' experience. Though one may discover the trait within the family, it is often not welcomed and those possessing the "abnormal" trait must typically learn their particular cultures from peers or at least outside of the family. They often cause parents to draw a line in the sand: *we* perceive ourselves to be normal and we have a child that is not normal. *We* often try to cure them.

I remember when I was first starting to allow cracks of queer light enter my consciousness. Homosexuality was still on the books as a disease in those days, and only a radical few had dared to think of it as an identity. They were especially hated by most of the mainstream, with lunchroom comments and op-ed musings like, "How dare they parade around. How dare they be proud?" I was desperate for a safe peer group that would help me find my way.

I sought solace in music. I remember listening over and over to Bronski Beat's "Why" and "Smalltown Boy" (both from the album *The Age of Consent*) before I was the age of consent. "The answers you seek will never be found at home …"

I remember my brother blurting out one day, "Bronski Beat? They're all fags."

I was mortified. I felt so ashamed yet also ablaze with a deep knowing as he brought this to my conscious awareness. From then on, I listened to them only on headphones or when my brother wasn't around.

Up until 1973, homosexuality was defined as a sociopathic personality disturbance in the Diagnostic and Statistical Manual of Mental Disorders (DSM). Researchers and psychologists, as well as religious organizations, tried to eradicate this illness. Countless billions of dollars have been spent trying to find the gene for homosexuality so we can cure it, or at least know whom to blame.

The number of gays and lesbians sent for aversion therapy will never be known due to shame, on the part of both the lesbians and gays and, more recently, the treatment providers. The practice existed from as early as the twenties up to very recently. In 1998, the American Psychological Association acknowledged the risk of aversion therapy. In some extremist religious groups, the practice still exists. The intention was, and still is, to eradicate this "illness." All aversion therapy sessions involved emotional harm and many included physical harm, such as electroshock treatment. One bizarre and disturbing treatment involved replacing the testicles of a homosexual man with the testicles from a deceased heterosexual. Exodus International, an organization committed to erasing homosexuality and filled with self-loathing "ex-homosexuals," did not get the exodus from the gay community that it hoped for and closed its doors in 2011. It ultimately apologized for the harm it had inflicted on countless gays and lesbians due to aversion therapy and other practices.

Meanwhile, *And Tango Makes Three* by Justin Richardson and Peter Parnell is one of the most-banned books in North America. It is a non-fiction children's book about two male penguins at the Central Park Zoo who are partners and try to hatch an egg-shaped rock until the zookeeper gives them an untended egg. The penguins care for it until it hatches and they become a family with their female offspring. Homosexuality can hardly be cast as a disease or a lifestyle choice under this circumstance, and the book lacks any moral condemnation for the penguins. Presumably, it is banned because it introduces homosexuality as an option to a young audience. *Please God, don't make my son queer!*

My twins are many things I am not, including gender normative. My daughter is a runner and a shopper. We can't and don't influence these things, except to open doors and provide encouragement. Recently my daughter, who is nine, started saying, "I hate gay couples" when she wants to pick a fight. Perhaps she will look to some of those gay couples for fashion mentorship, since she gets none at home.

Our daughter goes thrift store shopping with Nana (her foster mother) when we all get together, which is usually a couple of times a year. Our daughter returns with dress-up clothes: high heels, sparkly sweaters and a deep love that comes with having that side of her seen and celebrated. At the same time, our son rides on Papa's tractor or they build something together. We usually have dinner afterwards, all of us glowing with love for the twins. Inevitably, Nana and Papa tell us we are doing a great job and the children are lovely. They always make sure to ask how we are doing and whether we are taking care of our relationship. We are *all* in authentic relationships with each other, instead of relating to stereotypes of the Other.

The foster parents now raise chickens and grow flowers on their sunny bench. Nana feeds the chickens and collects eggs. I like to think that seeing the kids' smiles when we returned from our daily walks during our immersive adoption experience and hearing them talk enthusiastically about all our hikes since then has nudged Nana away from fear of an outdoor lifestyle. Maybe we've had a little something to do with that.

On one of these visits, I would like to ask the foster parents what they would do if their children grew up to be gay. I still ponder their question, "What will you do if your children grow up to be straight?" I believe our respective answers would be the same to both questions: love them, shine them up and celebrate their identities no matter what.

THE DIFFERENCE BETWEEN A HARD AND SOFT C

Nicole Breit

ONE

When I was sixteen, I fell in love with a sweet boy from school. Half Italian, half Dutch — shy brown eyes, a winsome smile.

At lunch we'd sit in the cafeteria. Compare words in the languages of his mother, my father.

Cognates — from a common root.

Six, zes, Sechs. Child, kind, Kind.

• • •

At twenty-one, startled by a crush on a sparkly redhead named Mariel from Russian class.

We practised writing our names in Cyrillic. Talked translations: Pasternak, Chekhov, Zoshchenko.

"You're not going to break up with me, are you?" my college boyfriend asks when I point her out at the party.

"No," I promise, "but isn't she gorgeous?"

• • •

The difference between women and men? The difference between a hard and soft C.

With men: catch, crave, consume.

With women: grace, cellular, necessary.

• • •

Beans: blue-green eyes with gold flecks. Straight blonde hair. Wide mouth, dimples. A quick wit, warm laugh.

We'd been friends since we were nine.

I stayed with her at night while her boyfriend worked the graveyard shift. Brought treats, rubbed her back with oil. She was grieving — her dad had recently died.

"I'll always take care of you," I said.

"You're sweet," she told me. "We'll take care of each other."

Over the next few months desire dawns on me slowly. Then, one night, I know.

We're at my apartment, lounging on my bed. The duvet cover a bright sunshine yellow covered in flowers.

I massage almond oil on her neck, shoulders. Say, "Turn over." Rub her chest — stroke her collarbone, the skin warming over her heart.

She closes her eyes, lips part slightly in a smile as she relaxes. I want to touch her everywhere.

Confess my feelings a few days later. She says, "Thank god it's not just me."

My friends worried when I told them. Asked, "Are you sure this is a good idea?"

· · ·

That summer she travelled to Germany with her boyfriend; a family reunion. When she returned we blew bubbles in an Italian restaurant. One landed on a pregnant woman who looked over and grinned.

I unlocked the door of my apartment. We stood at the threshold. Without a word I closed my eyes, kissed her.

Dropped the set of nesting dolls she brought me back from Poland. One mother inside another and another.

Watched the train wreck of her relationship unfold in slow motion as if it had nothing to do with me.

TWO

My co-worker of two years. First impression: handsome. The trace of an accent — he was from here, but his parents weren't.

We'd cut into the adjoining building for coffee. I was afraid he might be homophobic. But I was afraid everyone might be.

At the poster sale, Bob Marley smokes a reefer alongside Princess Leia, the slit in her white robe running all the way up her leg. Anne Geddes babies pop out of flower pots.

"Oh my god," I point to an arranged blonde and brunette kissing in their underwear. "It's me and Beans!" He laughs. Nods as he gets it.

When he asks about boyfriends, I say, "Yes, there have been some." But how to sum up a string of painful endings on a ten-minute coffee break?

He confesses he would marry two women if he could.

I tell him I wish I could marry a woman and a man — joking, not joking.

In a perfect world it would be legal to marry Beans. Our families would be happy.

And there'd be a man around when the mood struck.

• • •

"I've always wanted to be a mom," I tell Beans one afternoon in a coffee shop. She hasn't left her boyfriend yet, but I can see our future together.

"Me too," she smiles. We sit together in silence, holding hands. Holding on to that sweet possible-impossible thought.

She leaves him that fall. We keep talking.

Agree that neither of us imagines getting pregnant by artificial insemination. IUI, hCG, IVF — acronyms from an unromantic language we don't want to learn. Believe making a baby with the right man could be a beautiful adventure.

And of all the things we'll be accused of? Denying our child the chance to know their biological father won't be one of them.

We shortlist friends. A few flattered, intrigued. No takers.

• • •

My co-worker and I cross the bridge over the koi pond. A flock of geese fly overhead in a large V.

"Why didn't you think of me?" He sounds hurt. *Joking again,* I think.

"You'd give up your first-born?" I watch for non-verbal clues. His eyes remain earnest, serious.

"It's not like giving up my first-born. It's more like picking fruit from a tree."

I laugh.

"I don't want kids," he tells me. "You want to do this in a lab, right?"

I shake my head. "No, no weird science."

We walk back to the office under a thick, piny heat.

He offers to drive me home that night. Keeps his eyes on the road. Says, "I've never been with two women, but I don't think it's a problem. Three or four might be. There's only two of you, right?"

Honestly. I glance at him and smile; he grins back. The sun catches his eyes — almost reddish brown in the light.

A tiny fist punches me hard in the gut.

• • •

"He might be our best chance," I tell Beans when she walks in the door.

"Wow," she unbuckles her sandals, slides them off. "We'll have to think about it. Maybe have him over for drinks?"

"He thought we'd want to do it in a lab." I know this is a point in his favour. She raises an eyebrow.

"He's attractive, but can you imagine sleeping with him? He doesn't seem like your type." A serious question, but feigned skepticism means she's entertaining the idea, too.

It's true. Other men have been broke and artsy. Untucked flannel shirts, guitars and callouses, bedrooms that smell of oil paint.

But those kind brown eyes, a trace of vulnerability in them. The way he makes me laugh. He reminds me now of that first boy I loved.

I could imagine a threesome for the sake of a threesome.

THREE

A DIY weekend at home: Beans and I drink merlot, giggle, as we fashion burlesque pasties from marabou feathers, ribbons, glue.

"He has nice eyes," she concedes, "but I don't really know him. Honestly, there's no one I really think about but you."

I feel guilty, for liking him too much.

• • •

"Were you serious?" I instant message him one night after work. "What about the other ladies who want you?"

"They want something more expensive than genetic material." I imagine the straight face he is so good at. Then, "There's no one else I'd consider doing this with. Believe me, I'm thinking about it."

If he's the one, I think, *I could tell our child I loved the man who helped us have a baby.*

• • •

Beans lays beside me on the pink Tic-tac-toe square duvet. Kisses me all over with her soft lips. Fingertips almost imperceptible. Whispers that I look like an angel or a doll.

I lose my way in the Escher stairwells of the Academic Quadrangle. Know I'm with the right person — there is no one else I will love like this.

But I can't shake my dream:

I'm in a blue baby doll, he's in pyjamas. I feel the kiss through my whole body. Then we dissolve in a cyclone of colours.

Mad at myself for not being more straight or more gay — maybe, like Margaret Cho says, I'm just slutty.

Now, something harder. Biting. Penetration.

• • •

We can't talk at work. The nosy secretary who sits next to me smirks whenever he drops by my cubicle, brings me a latte.

According to HR, I'm a secretary, too. The new millennium and I'm asked to deliver my boss a sandwich for lunch.

Keepers of secrets? I look over at my neighbour as her long red nails clack the keyboard; hope it's true.

MSN messenger, our new evening routine.

"I need to know what you're thinking," I type. "Do I need to go to the liquor store and download eighties power ballads?"

"I can see it now — our baby. I need a bit more time."

I hold my breath, wondering how far he's already travelled in his thoughts.

"If it's yes, can you make us feel beautiful?" I try to hold back; hit send.

His instant reply: "That part, my friend, is easy."

• • •

We make a date to talk after work on Christmas Eve. Months since that first conversation when the weather was warm. Even in cool temperatures, flashes of red-gold koi darting around the grey pond.

I boil a pot of tea. He taps a leg under the table. Speaks quietly when I press.

"I'm sorry, I can't do it. It's too big a secret to keep. And I'm not sure I could detach."

Beans comes home. Is cheerful when she sees us eating shortbread cookies.

"Hi!" I tell her his decision so he doesn't have to.

"Of course," she says and smiles graciously. "Thank you for even considering it."

He gets up to leave; I sense his sadness that he's letting us down. I'm sad, too, but also grateful.

At the door I touch his shoulders, turn him around so I can hug him. Beans hugs him, too.

Some words have a hard and soft C. Some have neither.

Chemistry, chaos. Child.

FOUR

In the new year, we regroup. Time not wasted; a step forward. A test of what we're willing to try.

Try to ignore the sound of clocks, ticking.

"It's been a good thing, don't you think?" I ask as we sip Pinot Gris in the bubble bath.

"I guess so," she says. "But what if I don't want to be with someone and you do? I want you to have what you want. But I also feel scared."

I say I'll never want another woman. But I do think about him.

At meetings: crisp pin-striped shirts, top button undone. On the drive home, afternoon stubble.

"Maybe I should get to know him better," she suggests. "But I don't think I'll ever catch up to you two. You see each other every day."

Friday morning coffee: he and I circle the Academic Quadrangle alongside students milling to class, white noise all around us. I stall on the way back. Chest, neck, cheeks blotch with heat.

"I dreamed about you last night."

He slows his pace; wants to know if my dream was prophetic.

"I pushed you against a wall."

"Really?" He takes a sip, meets my eye. "You should try it."

"But you wouldn't kiss me on the lips." My subconscious never lies about motives. Feelings.

"Try it," he says. "Push me."

· · ·

On the drive home we talk like we always do. Laugh about Kenny Rogers, code name for my boss.

He pulls up to the curb. We stop talking.

I unlock the front door. Clang of metal keys on the counter. Slap of blinds closing. Click of heels across the tile to where he watches me from the threshold.

Two palms flat against his chest. One firm push. A fiery look, flash of light in his eyes — half surprised — as he collides with the door.

He grips my waist, pulls me close. A hard-soft kiss on the mouth. Like a blind dive in a deep pool.

A new ache begins sometime between my hands unbuckling his belt and his fingers on my skin, unclasping my bra.

My mind a pale sheet. His mouth hot on my neck, weight pressing me to the floor.

I want to cry. It is beautiful and terrible to know.

Tell him we have to stop. He rolls off, stands up. I watch him button his rumpled dress shirt, tuck it in his jeans.

For days this ache will persist. Deep inside the place where the child with brown eyes, a mind for possibilities and a heart like mine — capable of selfishness but also love — won't grow.

• • •

I tell her while she's shaving her legs in the tub. Careful, contrite.

We don't break up. Instead, drink beer until four in the morning.

Watch *Meet the Parents*. Laugh cathartically when Ben Stiller hits his sister-in-law in the face with an aggressive serve and the pool fills with blood.

I walked to the liquor store after he left. For courage and a chance at forgiveness, brought home a six pack and bottle of cinnamon whiskey.

"What did you want?" she wants to know. I take her fingers in my mouth. Suck, swirl, pull.

Ignore his email the next day: Are you okay? Is she? Please let me know.

My hair drips in strands as I stand, head bowed, all weekend. Hot shower. Cold shower.

Beans says she isn't mad. She needs time, though, to figure out what she feels. Stays in her pyjamas under the covers until Sunday night reading *Paris 1919*.

I'm a child's top. Wound so tight I can't spin. Try to make myself come but I can't.

• • •

Back at work we go for coffee. I ask, "Is this painful tension what it's like for guys all the time?"

He stares. "Really? You feel that way?"

Two weeks later, blood. Of course. I was ovulating that full-moon Friday.

As I screw in the new IKEA shelves, I come across a quote by Molière — that master of French tragicomedies.

A postcard Beans sent me from her trip to Europe with the man she left for me.

The pleasure of love is in change.

FIVE

Love for a woman, desire for a man — not apples and oranges. Chardonnay and crème brûlée.

"At first I was jealous, but I went for a walk and decided I just need to deal with my feelings. I love you. I don't want to lose you," she says.

I'm humbled by her love. Shamed by how much I am asking for — how much it takes to be taken as I am. That she, my patient girlfriend, is willing to try.

"I'm sorry. I don't want it to happen again, but I can't pretend I don't feel this way. And I won't lie to you."

She doesn't want me to make promises I can't keep. Worries she'll end up a fool.

I felt the same way for six months waiting for her to leave her boyfriend. But it feels manipulative, impolite, to bring this up.

• • •

A friend lends me her copy of *The Ethical Slut*.

Polyamory. From the Greek root word for several, Latin for love.

I read it and think, *Yes, yes, yes.*

It is possible to have more than one consensual intimate relationship; other people do it. Maybe this is all about different needs being met.

Or a heart, not deviant, but big enough to love more than one person; one gender.

Then the clamp tightens back down. Isn't it enough to be bi? Do I have to be polyamorous, too? A member of two sexual minorities?

No matter what I do, people will look at me and think, *Selfish.*

And if the time ever comes? *Terrible mother.*

• • •

Beans and I are pre-approved for a mortgage.

The next step in our motherhood master plan? A two-bedroom townhouse.

We'll replace whatever needs to be replaced. Fix whatever needs to be fixed.

On the day we get the keys I turn thirty-one. Officially older than my mom was when she had me.

A gorgeous orchid in a blue flowerpot from Beans — fragile. I'm afraid I'll kill it.

We celebrate with friends in the pub. I squeeze her thigh. We leave the table, make out in a bathroom stall. Fall out the door laughing.

Beans reads *The Ethical Slut*, too.

"I understand it intellectually," she says. "Maybe I just have to get used to the idea of you being with someone else."

"This is like the Quebec Referendum," I say. "Voting again and again until we get to *Yes*."

"*Oui*," she says.

SIX

Lindsay on *Queer as Folk* cheats with a man. The air turns cool in the living room. I can feel Beans' disappointment that she can't resist.

• • •

He drives me home from work; a semi pulls up beside us at the intersection. The driver looks down, sees my hand sliding up his thigh. "Busted," he says, waiting for the light to turn green.

• • •

In the bath I help her shave her legs. "You look pretty," she says. A relaxed smile.

"But I am also devilish." Confess that I touched his cheek, stroked his leg in the car.

She looks at the razor I'm holding in my hand. I put it on the edge of the tub.

"I didn't kiss him. He didn't touch me."

"Don't be sorry," she says, getting out. Drying off.

Sex. Admitted later we were both thinking about him.

"It's not that I want him romantically. It's different," I say.

"It's sweet to imagine you touching him in the car. But if we come to an agreement, do I give up my right to feel jealous?"

As we paint over the tan walls with Vermont Cream, put away our clothes and books, things feel more orderly.

But I'm like a vase with an invisible fissure. Fill me up to the top but I'll never stay full.

. . .

I want to know how we are ever going to have a baby if we can't work through this.

"We can't let fear drive us," I say one evening as we read together in bed.

"I think you should sleep with him." Her tone is gentle but firm. Like she's giving me advice that is for my own good.

I don't know what to say. Look at her. Try to tell if I've finally lost her.

"But this isn't how I thought it would be," she says. "I thought two people who love each other didn't need anyone else."

Love, friendship, sex — categorical boundaries that blur so easily for me. But I can distinguish my feelings.

I want to say I will never have fantasies of lazy weekend brunches with him or raising children together.

But no perfect combination of words can change the way someone feels.

"You won't lose me," I say.

It's like telling someone ghosts don't exist so they feel less afraid — even though you, yourself, believe they do.

The difference? You know they can't hurt you.

SEVEN

A warm August night. Second full moon. Tourmaline sky.

Beans at the cabin. Reading true crime on the deck as the sun sets in the cove.

I sit in the passenger seat of his car; feel like if I start laughing I won't stop. Think, *I can leave right now. I could open the door, walk home alone.*

"I can never just buy condoms," he tells me as he slides into the driver's seat. "I bought toothpaste, too."

"I have toothpaste at home," I say with a straight face.

He turns up the hip hop, sexy rhythmic beats, on the drive back.

Not eighties power ballads — our joke when he and I first started talking about donors. The key to virility, stamina.

• • •

I fix him a martini, pour myself a glass of wine in the kitchen. Show him the bedroom down the hall we've painted butter yellow. The baby's room, we hope.

"Wow," he says, when I flick on the light in the master bedroom. A blinding pink ricochets around the room.

"They call this colour Vibrato." I look down at my feet and laugh. Sense how close he's standing — a brush of bicep along my arm.

"Touch my face," he takes my hand. "I didn't shave for you."

"It's a blue moon." I stall, wondering when, how long ago, I told him what I liked. Stroke his cheek, close my eyes. Then: a slow, deep kiss.

"You're so pretty. Can I take your clothes off?" He checks again when I say yes. "Are you sure?"

I let him peel my jeans down my legs. Trace the tattoo on my right hip that marked the end of men.

Tell him what I want; feel his urgency as he unwraps a condom. Then, a dawning frustration.

"It's the alcohol," he apologizes. "It happens sometimes with some-one new."

"It's okay," I say. But slow-deep-hard is the only way to touch the ache that's been with me for months.

It gets late. Eventually I come the way I always do: underneath a warm body, my legs wrapped tight around his. Pushing up, up, up; clinging.

EIGHT

Late summer. A new job, new office to myself on the opposite side of campus. The other side of the koi pond; everywhere you look, lush green flora.

A tiny photo of me and Beans taped to my monitor. Bright yellow flower painting from last year's poster sale tacked to my wall.

The baby question on hold while we figure out our next move.

• • •

A cooling autumn afternoon. After hours, I call. Ask him to meet me in the café.

Fifteen minutes later I'm ignoring my tea. Shifting in my seat. Can't take in what he's saying.

I watch his mouth; stare at his jaw. Want to feel the roughness on my fingertips again, his five o'clock shadow. When he gets up I reach for his sleeve.

He doesn't say a word. Follows me down the stairs, past the open door where a colleague stares, unblinking, at her blue screen.

I let him in, turn the lock, turn toward him. His hands land on my shoulders. Mouth on mine, presses my body to the wall.

"I want to touch you," he says. Slides his hands down my dress. My skin warms; neurons shoot sparks.

He sits on my office chair, pulls me gently onto his lap. I drag my mouth along his bristly cheek. Lips swell, tingle. Breathe in his clean skin — cedar, sandalwood.

"What do you want?" He kisses my neck, collarbone.

"Oh god. Do you have anything?" Not a baby. Not now, not like this.

He murmurs something I can't hear. My ears full of the sound of my pounding heart.

My mind reduces to a pinpoint focus. I become small; hard and round. Move without thinking. Slide dress up, wrap legs around his belted waist; rock, hard.

His mouth over my ear; says it again.

I smash into the ceiling; crash back down into my body. Deep shuddery breaths. He doesn't let me go until I stop shaking.

Slide off his lap, kneel on the floor. Stroke him along the zipper of his jeans. "Let me, I want to," I say. But he takes my hand. "No, Honey."

I was wrong about what could reach that ache. Six words no man has ever said to me. *I want to make you come.*

• • •

When I unlock the office door, I feel the change. Subtle, like his scent on my fingertips.

Fading light, the black curtain falling. He turns to me on the sidewalk. "You're flushed," he smiles. "Covered in pretty dust."

I bump into him as we cross the road; light-headed. He leaves me at the bus stop under a street lamp. Braces himself against the chill as he makes his way back to his office.

On the ride home I stand near the front doors; hold onto the pole for balance. Try to think of the words I'll use. I have no idea.

But I have to tell her. So she knows she can trust me.

NINE

A week later his message pops up when Beans logs on to our computer.

"There's something I need to know."

She calls over her shoulder, "Your work boyfriend wants to talk to you."

"Ignore him," I say. Sign in later when I hear her run a bath down the hall.

"There's something I need to know," he types. "Are you in love with me?"

He told me he loved me once. I'd asked him over for coffee after work. We were talking about the art class he was taking. My floor hockey team, The Red Hot Mamas.

I was in the kitchen, he was in the dining room. I thought he was being sweet, vocalizing a fleeting thought.

Always careful about crossing boundaries — even in my dream he wouldn't kiss me first. I was the one to break the tension by pushing him against a wall.

"I love you, too," I smiled, and meant it. Set down two cups and a plate of cookies. He left a short time later; lingered quietly for a moment at the door.

Now my heart kicks in; panic. Fingers miss keys, backspace.

"No," I type. "But if you were in love with me would you tell me?"

"I love you," he types back. "I would tell you."

Ellipses in the dialogue box show he's still thinking, still typing. Before I can respond a new message appears.

"No, I wouldn't. Admitting it would make me feel weak."

I feel it, then. *Liebe und Angst.* Love and dread — two emotions running parallel, simultaneously.

Everything tied up about to unravel. A darkening cloud, from far away so lovely — now, falling.

I sign out, stay offline. Work the next few days with my door closed.

. . .

Winter, a few years later. The evening is dark, snow on the ground. I can see my breath; small white puffs dissolve in front of me as I cross campus, rushing to meet Beans after work.

Am I remembering this right? That I was pushing the baby in the stroller — or was I alone?

This I remember clearly: I catch sight of him at the last moment, too late to return his glance. A glimpse of his face. Composed. A smile; amused, maybe.

He shakes his head as we pass each other like he's remembering something he can't believe.

Something crazy. A cosmic coincidence.

. . .

When it's over with him, a new start. I always believed a third didn't have to destroy us.

The beauty of outsider privileges: we make our own rules.

Together we search for someone we both want. Pursue the dream with more insight. More wisdom.

Sit together at the computer, two umbrella drinks. Homemade cosmopolitans. Choose the sepia photo taken the previous summer for our online dating profile.

Wild, wild west. Corsets, ruffled skirts hiked up to reveal cash in our garter belts. Back to back on the bar, holding rifles.

Come closer. But don't mess with us.

Daydream that among the many men who send us a wink or a note — as near as Vancouver, as far as North Dakota — one of them is the father of our child.

A word that connotes imagination, evokes wonder — the future. A word with a hard and soft C.

Conceive.

THIS ROAD

Eamon MacDonald

"I'm honoured and bewildered. I'm happy and I need to think about this."

Your parting words echo through my mind as I pull away from the curb for the three-hour drive home. *What a perfect reaction*, I think. I smile at the thought of you and of our friendship, at the thought of what might be ahead for us. As I shift gears and merge lanes onto the highway, I imagine you heading back to your office with new thoughts to consider. I think of our slow and easy conversation on this late fall day. I switch on the windshield wipers and settle in for the drive, contemplating a future I can barely imagine. How can I feel so peaceful and so excited at the same time?

And then I wait.

Weeks go by. November becomes December and then January. No word. I am so determined not to put any pressure on you, determined to give you the time you need to mull this one over, to convince yourself it is a good thing.

Finally, I break. I make the call that I've been waiting to make. And I hear you, discouraged. I know you. I've known you for more than a dozen years now, since we were teenagers. I know how you hate to disappoint other people. It's not you who doesn't want this; it's your lover, you tell me. He's not sure that this would work, and he's not wanting it in any case. As for you, you want this, but you would never push him. And that's you also — not one to put yourself first; definitely one to take others into account.

It could have worked, I think. *He's wrong*. But I can't, and wouldn't, and don't say this.

I am on the couch in your apartment on a hot July evening. More than a year has gone by. I listen this time to your heart, breaking at the loss of your lover. He has found someone else. You share only so much, and after you've said what you need to say, we work together to keep the conversation on a lighter plane. We have a history of student politics, shared music and mutual friends. We've driven down highways together, singing Bette Midler, Neil Young and Joni Mitchell. We've handed out pamphlets together and listened to new albums together. We've sat through a hundred or more meetings on economic policy and post-secondary funding. I've watched you in your job as a summer camp counsellor, dripping fistfuls of mud into sandcastle spires, children piled around you. I am your friend. I hate that your heart is hurting. I hate to know you feel so betrayed.

I don't mention pregnancy and you don't ask. I have found a donor — an earnest, sensitive and lovely man, a friend of a friend. I barely know him, but he seemed generous and interested when the possibility had been introduced to him. But it's been more than a year of trying and nothing is happening. I want for it all to matter less, to be prepared to let the hope of a child go.

Months and months later. April. The donor has long since moved to a new city. There have been a couple of other possible donors, each with his own complications. I am in a new relationship, and she is supportive but distant and unsure. Her own children are nearly grown. I am beginning to wonder whether I should persist. My life is happy, but pregnancy may not be the only path, or even the right one. There is another direction for myself that I have been denying. This is something I have shared with nearly no one, not even you. I could have a child, I have told myself. It's the one thing that this female body of mine can do that might make sense of the fact that I was born female. Or, I could begin the road to transition. I could walk away from one and walk toward the other. It all feels complex and overwhelming.

I am in my small kitchen when the phone rings. You are coming through town later in the day. "Shall we have dinner tonight?" Yes, absolutely.

For fun, I pull out my deck of tarot cards before I meet you — not seriously, but they make me think of you, of the late nights we had spent with my guitar and your piano, or of the long car rides we took when we were first just getting to know each other. We had been university students then, drifting, both of us. Now in our thirties, we have serious jobs and responsibilities. I lay out the cards and turn each one over. They all make sense. The final outcome of the question I had posed: the Sun card, a child, full of light, a celebration, a beginning. Hope, optimism, movement. This road.

The gay bar is a block from my house and serves meals. I meet you there. Midway through our dinner, you ask whether I still have that plan, whether I am still wanting a child.

Yes.

Yes. And you also answer yes. Yes, despite the disapproval of your doctor, a gay man himself, who nevertheless does not believe that gay men should enter into family planning. Yes, despite the worry you must have that your heart could be broken again. Yes, and trusting that we can work this out.

I have thought so much of this through, and this is what I say I want: "I want, at a minimum, for you to be willing to be a known donor, if the child should have any questions at any point.

"And I want, at a maximum, something less than 50 per cent from you — I want the child to have one home and for that home to be with me. There can be constant visits and weekends with you or weeks in the summer, but I want there to be a principal home, and for me to be in it.

"And between that minimum and maximum, I want for you to figure out what you want and then be willing to stay with it — not to disappear or to suddenly demand much more. I want there to be some consistency in the child's life, home and family arrangements.

"And what I will offer is that I will respect whatever choice you make and wherever you set your own needs or limits, and that I will support your relationship with the child, whatever shape you want that to take. You can just be a donor, or you can be a parent. You can involve your family, or not. You choose."

And what you want, what you choose, is to be involved. You want a relationship with the child. You want your parents to be grandparents and your siblings to be aunts and uncles. You want to be able to be around — for birthdays and holidays and the occasional weekend, for a week in the summer and for a few hours every week.

Why you?

We had known each other at this point for sixteen years. There was trust, which would end up being an extraordinary relief for me, much later, when I would feel so very vulnerable at times. I also knew you loved children. When you came out I was there for you, and I knew that, while coming out was a wonderful, freeing realization of your desire, it had also come with some grief knowing that you would never have children. Among all of the gay men I knew at the time, you were unique in that regard — your desire for a family. We had worked together many times. We had campaigned together during election time, organized campus political events together, sat together on provincial and national student committees, sung and played at coffee houses together, laughed together and talked late into the night. I had listened, rapt, during the nights when you lost yourself at the keyboard, churning out musical improvisations for hours, pausing only occasionally for a sip of a drink or a drag of smoke. You were sweet and gentle and thoughtful and kind.

I remember once, during the first few years when we were still getting to know each other: it was late evening, dark outside, and you were in your car when you saw me. I was walking down a side street. You didn't honk or wave or do anything that might have startled or frightened a woman walking alone in the dark at night. Instead, you pulled over and got out and stood away from the car, facing me, your arms away from your sides, your palms facing out, and only then did you call out a greeting. You looked so vulnerable in that moment. I knew it was you immediately.

And so, the process began.

May — You got all the necessary tests, withstanding your doctor's vehement disapproval.

June — Pride in Toronto. Seemed like a promising occasion, yet there was a shadow hovering: you had attended three funerals in the previous few weeks. All gay men, all your age. Among dozens over the last few years. You had lost count. And still we made our first attempt, both awkward and comfortable. The condom, the syringe, the jar.

July — Another visit to Toronto. I spent the day in your apartment while you were at work, afterwards taking the three-hour bus ride home.

August — It is suddenly real.

A hot August morning. I rise early and take the pregnancy test kit to the bathroom. I wait the next few minutes to read it.

Yes.

I return to my lover in bed. She's awake already. I tell her.

"It's over," she says. "I can't do this."

We cry, and we talk. There had been no warning, no signal and no indication because she hadn't wanted to deprive me of this hope, this choice. And because she rightly knew that, had I known how she felt, I would have stopped trying. I was that happy with us. I was that in love.

But her feelings for me relied on seeing me as the person I also understood myself to be: not female, not a woman. And she could not be in a relationship with someone who was pregnant, someone who was a mother. She had counted on this never happening.

I had just moved into her house. I would have to move out, she says. We could wait until the baby is born, she offers. I was working two jobs at the time, one in town and one in a city two hours away.

"But I need you to be out of here. Before the baby is three months old. I can't do this."

I wept then. We wept and wept.

Together and apart.

I feel so alone.

I call you that night. The news comes as a surprise to you. I have been expecting this, after more than twenty months of trying. And yet my own optimism and joy has just been smashed. All I could feel was despair and loss — the loss of my relationship, the loss of my home.

For you, this is sudden — just the second month of trying — and your excitement and hopefulness is unalloyed.

You are at your family's land on a beautiful lake. It is a clear, dark night. You tell me the next day that, after our call, you had gone down to the dock and lain on it for a long time looking at the stars, and it had come to you with absolute certainty that the child would be a girl.

The months of pregnancy are a blur. Too much work and too many emotions. Deep grief and horrible confusion. My relationship with my lover is on briefly again and then it is off. I am more dysphoric than ever. I don't recognize myself in the mirror. I have dreams in which I can't figure out who I am. I have a dream in which the baby has only a head, no body, and the nurse attaches the head to a filing cabinet. What the hell is that about?

I wonder daily if I have made the worst mistake of my life. I don't know how to feel. I wear baggy clothes. People still regularly presume I'm male. In the ninth month of pregnancy, strangers still sometimes call me Sir. I don't know where this is going, but I do know, I am profoundly sure, that I am utterly committed to this child, to being a good parent.

And you, you are steady and friendly and respectful. You tell your family and they are surprised and happy and hopeful for you and for themselves, that they will have a new family member to celebrate. Mostly, they need to know that I will honour their and your relationship with this child.

I tell my family. They are sure I have ruined my life and committed a deep injustice to the child, because of my "lifestyle." I don't bother telling them about the crisis in my relationship. They know nothing of my other identity struggles. I am sure they wouldn't care. They suggest, bizarrely, that you and I should hold a ceremony to commit to each other.

I don't need a ceremony, but you have no idea how much I rely on you being you, on your trustworthiness. You cannot imagine how much I need you to keep being you.

I am in labour. I am well along when I finally decide to call you and, even then, I tell you to take your time. I don't even know if I will want you in the delivery room. Half an hour later, just after midnight, the contractions are intense, and my ex-lover, her old friend who is visiting and I head for the hospital. Hours after that, at the end of your three-hour drive, you arrive to find me anguished, in deep pain. The labour is fast — really fast, and beyond intense. I have given you instructions that, whatever is going on, you are to stay with the baby until all is well.

And so, you do. You see her being born. You are there, and so are my former lover and the nurse, and then finally, just before her birth, the doctor.

She comes into the world squalling and wildly alive. And utterly and absolutely perfect. I am overcome with love.

We have brought champagne to the hospital to celebrate. It is seven in the morning, and I am exhausted but thirsty. I am deeply humbled and joyful. The three of us — you, my ex-partner and I — down our glasses of bubbly and celebrate.

Later in the day, my parents arrive. You graciously greet them and join them for dinner. Later again, you drop by the hospital to say goodnight, and then head for the gay bar. The bartender asks how you are. "Ecstatic," you tell him.

All of that was a long time ago.

We have a wonderful daughter, in her mid-twenties now.

And things are different, as they always are.

I couldn't have known or guessed where all of this would go.

I didn't realize how much you would become my family as well as my friend. How could I not have seen this?

I didn't know the grief you would go through: the death of one partner, just six years after our daughter was born, the one you had met while I was pregnant. And then, incomprehensibly, the death many years later of your beloved husband, the one you met when our daughter was nine. He had, in his own way, loved and parented our girl. His family, too, had come to see her as theirs.

I didn't know how much it would come to mean to you to be a father, nor how much you would mean to her. And you do mean so very much. Both of you to each other.

I didn't know that the divergent paths of pregnancy and transition that I felt I would need to choose between would weave together again. Now I find myself in a community where my trans-ness is welcomed, where I can be both myself and somehow also a mother.

I didn't know that my partner at the time would struggle for a few years longer with the ambiguity of our relationship before finally letting go and moving on.

I didn't know that I would have another long relationship with someone, now a dear friend, who would herself come to be our daughter's family and mine.

Nor did I foresee that I would begin a relationship with an old friend of mine who is also, coincidentally, an old friend of yours, from more than four decades ago. And so, our family shapes and reshapes itself. And it will continue to do so.

I might have guessed but did not know that our daughter would be welcomed both into your family and into mine with love and generosity and joy.

What I do know is that there are a lot of ways to be friends and a lot of ways to be family. I do know that I am so deeply grateful for what we have, for our daughter, for you, for the choices you made and for what you have given me — for what we have given each other.

Like a Boy, but Not a Boy
One Experience of Non-binary Pregnancy

andrea bennett

As my left leg bumps the edge of the coffee table, a small wave of coffee curls up the side of the mug. Always clumsy, I seem to have lost all sense of the boundaries of my body over the course of the last few months. The apartment I share with my partner, Will, is a small 3 ½ located in Little Italy in Montreal. Will is an avid gardener and lately, the *Dracaena marginata* (which we call Margie VII), perched precariously on top of a Go board in the living room, is my greatest nemesis: I've knocked it off its centre and caught it as it's fallen an average of once a week.

It is odd to have lost grip of where I end and the world begins. It's odd and bruising in a different way that the world has lost sense of my conceptual boundaries, too. Last week I was on St-Viateur in Mile End taking photos for a guidebook I'm writing, and I walked past a man and woman heading in the opposite direction. The woman said in French, speaking to the man but looking directly at me, "You think they are boys and then they are not boys."

I've been thinking a lot about when Kim Kardashian was pregnant with North and the entire tabloid press was obsessed with her weight gain. My jeans got tight at six weeks along; when I went to a maternity store to find new pants, I lied and said I'd reached nine. Size was not the only way in which I felt like an imposter: it seemed as though all the clothing on offer wished to emphasize every bit of body I generally try to downplay. Boob shelves, bows, florals; form-fitting and empire-waist dresses. In the back, on the discount rack, I found two dark-coloured pairs of stretchy skinny jeans. They'd do; I'd find shirts in the men's section at the various thrift stores in our neighbourhood.

On Instagram, I follow two different kinds of accounts that allow me to see parts of myself reflected back at me. I follow accounts that celebrate curvy bodies; these overwhelmingly feature feminine women. Stripped of clothes, the outline of my body resembles aspects of the variety of shapes and sizes that pass through my feed. Yet I also follow accounts that display transmasculine and tomboy style. In clothes, this is what I want my body to look like. If I only followed these latter accounts, I might find my naked outline wanting. I might pine for a smooth swimmer's triangle of a body. I might feel even more enmity vis-à-vis my breasts than I currently do. (The day I found out I was pregnant, I was excited for two reasons: in addition to the pregnancy itself, I'd also made the decision to delay relieving myself permanently of breasts until I had and nursed a kid — pregnancy lit the gas lamp at the end of that particular tunnel.) I know that many masculine-of-centre people have bodies like mine; nonetheless, I sometimes can't help but feel that the shape of my body betrays me to onlookers.

Our culture is currently into bodies like Kim Kardashian's — into them until they cross a line; into them until the same tendencies that allow for curves lead to monstrous pregnancies. My own body has felt monstrous since it began to fit nowhere, exactly. The monstrousness of pregnancy came as no great shock or surprise; I knew to pay more attention to pregnancies that reflected genders more like my own back at me. I understood not to take personally the aesthetic directions of the clothing at the maternity store. The two little lines on the stick showed up nearly two decades after I'd set thinness, femininity and girlhood aside and decided to accept myself for who I was.

I grew up in a suburb outside Hamilton and I've been a gender non-conformist since I was a kid. This so deeply disappointed one of my parents that it was part of the reason I had to learn to live without her love.

I always felt a bit like a boy, but not really like a boy. I always had crushes on boys, even as I found most of them wanting. I started Googling "straight butch?" as soon as I hit university and met queer friends. Later, thanks to Tumblr, I came across the term *non-binary*, and it clicked into place like an overall buckle over its button. By the time Will and I met, I'd learned to negotiate relationship-related gender issues one by one. I knew to seek out softer men who wanted what I wanted: to strike a balance where we were both close to the middle of the gender teeter-totter. But I was scared, even with Will, when I decided to tell him that I wouldn't always have breasts. "Fw-wssht," I said, curling my hand up and away.

"How do you see me?" I had asked him once. He said he saw me like I'd once described the way I saw myself: a person, first and foremost. I knew this was a privilege the rest of the world wouldn't afford me, just as it does not afford others, but I was relieved and full of gratitude to have it in my own home, in my own relationship.

When Will and I got married, we wrote gender-neutral vows and both wore suits. We explained to our families that I wouldn't be going by bride or wife — we'd be sticking with "partner." We had a small casual wedding three months after deciding to get married. It all, language-wise, went fine enough.

When I got pregnant two and a half years later, I was reminded of my family's initial reaction when I told them Will and I were getting married: they'd never expected me to. Though no one had ever really verbalized that they'd seen my gender non-conformity, not *exactly*, it was clear that they had seen it by their reaction. They'd seen it and read it as a rejection of everything they associated with heteronormative gender roles. Getting married was a blip on one's life timeline, but pregnancy and parenthood was a much larger commitment — a much larger commitment that my family, like perhaps a lot of families, see as the next step in a row of conventionally heteronormative choices.

I'd been thinking of raising a kid in the context of my partnership with Will, where the two of us would share parenting and working, as we share everything else. To the world outside my relationship, though, a gestational parent coupled with a cis male partner immediately reinscribed woman — and motherhood — it immediately reinscribed a gender, and its role, that no one who knew me well would ever have prescribed to me.

Is this a problem of body, or language? I wondered.

I first broached the "I'm not Mom" conversation with my brother and dad while visiting them right after Will and I told them I was pregnant. We were sitting in a restaurant booth in a town at the tip of the Bruce Peninsula. I was irritably hungry, and I'd just ordered nachos.

My brother, close in age and relationship but far away in life experience, wore a now-familiar look of mild confusion.

"But you call me Dad, and that's gendered," my dad said.

And so it was, at thirty-two, that I began to experience the raft of questions, comments and concerns one receives when one comes out. (Like, for example, "Not everyone will understand as well as me," and "You know that this is going to make things harder for you?" etc.)

As I floated ideas about what I might prefer as an alternative to Mom or Dad — Zaza, Omma, Momo — well-meaning family members shot down each and every one.

Every time I feel I've made headway, we backslide. I try to remember to feel lucky to have family that loves us, family who wants to try to understand, but the power of the pregnancy-female-mother connection is strong enough as to efface all efforts.

At my lowest points — hormonal and physically exhausted — I feel myself wilt like an unwatered, thirsty plant. I give up trying to find an alternative. The truth is, I'm not an early adopter; if I could, I'd give in, melt myself down and reform as mother. But I can't do that, either. So, I'll be, simply, a *parent*. Instead of telling the kid to call me Mom, I'll ask them to call me by my first name. I'll ask the kid and I'll ask my family — I'll ask and hope they'll listen.

By nineteen weeks, I have felt the fetus flutter a couple times: once when leaning a little too hard against the kitchen counter doing dishes; another time lifting a heavy box of bike parts up onto a shelf at a bike co-op where I've started volunteering. But mostly I feel nothing, and it worries me. When I was first pregnant, I Googled rates of miscarriage by age and the statistics were not extraordinarily comforting. I wrote in a poem that the world had been lying — there *was* such a thing as "a little bit pregnant." I began to talk about being pregnant before conventional wisdom says you're supposed to, and Will and I made a tour of the area's thrift stores, buying and washing onesies and sweaters with creature themes. The anxiety passed momentarily after the first ultrasound, but it came back shortly after: it was statistically unlikely but still possible that something could go wrong. I could have this belly and then I could have a child, or I could have this belly and then it could deflate before any of the strangers I pass in the street even realize I'm plump *with child.*

I do not feel dysphoric in my pregnant body. I feel different anxieties — anxieties about loss and death, primarily — but I do not feel dysphoric in my body. I feel dysphoric in the *language used* to talk about my body, my pregnant body.

By twenty-two weeks, I need but refuse to buy a larger bra, hoping, like goldfish, they will only grow to the size of the bowl they're given.

By thirty weeks, I have both insomnia and some new tactics for approaching well-meaning loved ones who keep referring to me as Mom and Momma. My dad has taken to talking about my pregnancy by underscoring that he's looking forward to being a grand*parent*, not a grand*father*; baffled and annoyed, I tell him what I'd appreciate more is if he could expend some of that energy telling his friends *my* wishes when it comes to names and terms and roles. "He's trying," Will says.

I decide that when we send thank-you cards — our families and friends have been so kind and supportive in so many ways, sending notes and gifts as the due date approaches — we can introduce the baby's name and reinforce the parent terms we'll use all at once.

Outside of the heavily gendered French-language healthcare system (where it takes enough mental effort to understand directives speaking in my second language), I will begin gently employing a script I have prepared to correct a friend, family member or stranger's use of "Mom." I will start buying picture books that display a variety of different family structures so that, hopefully, my own home will continue to be a place where I can easily and without friction be myself. Up until now, I've been doing a simultaneous rewrite, in my head, of all the pregnancy literature so that it includes me. If I need to, I'll write and draw the books myself.

Though I've never knocked over Margie VII, Will's prize *Dracaena marginata*, our cat has felled her on two separate occasions. Margie's pot bears a series of cracks and fissures; part of it has been reinforced with folded tinfoil. Every time the cat knocks over one of Will's plants — he deeply loves the cat; he deeply loves the plants — he feels mad at the cat. Then he superglues the pot back together; lovingly replants Margie, or Phil, or whomever else has been affected; sweeps up the debris; and forgives the cat. This whole exercise is a useful metaphor. I could wish for a simple wholeness that betrays no cracks or fissures, but I will be better served by learning to pick myself up and heal as many times as necessary.

THE BIRTH VIDEO

Rachel Epstein

It seems I can't go anywhere in queer community without meeting someone who has seen a close-up of my pregnancy hemorrhoids.

I gave birth at home in 1992, surrounded by an eleven-person birth team. Each team member had a task: two queer midwives and my partner (at the time) and co-parent, Lois, headed the team, while others timed contractions and provided snacks and meals. There was an assigned communications officer and, importantly, a bouncer — the person I could inform if I wanted anyone or everyone to leave. All of this was captured on video by my friend Amy, who was in charge of documentation.

Hundreds of people would end up seeing an edited version of this video of my labour and Sadie's birth, as part of the Dykes Planning Tykes (DPT) course — a Toronto-based course for queer women considering parenthood, developed in 1997 by Kathie Duncan, the midwife who caught Sadie, and me. Twenty years later the course still runs and many of the course participants are now parents.

The first run of the DPT course, sponsored by the Centre for Lesbian and Gay Studies, was held at the University of Toronto's International Student Centre on St. George Street. Kathie and I decided it might be helpful for people, many of whom would be either giving birth themselves or supporting someone in labour, to see what a human birth looks like. We edited the five hours Amy had filmed down to twenty-five minutes and shared this version during the first course. After that, it became a standard part of the course curriculum.

In my opinion, mine is a reassuring labour. There is no screaming, and nothing goes wrong. I appear calm despite the pain of contractions, and I am surrounded by love. The midwives are lovely and competent and appreciative of all the support in the room.

The *Birth Video*, as it came to be known, was shown on the last night of the course. Each time I introduced it, I felt a little embarrassed. Who shows a video of themselves giving birth as part of a course they are teaching? I feared looking like an attention-seeking egomaniac. But then, what attention-seeking egomaniac shows a video of themselves exhausted in full-term pregnancy, walking up and down a hallway wearing nothing but an unflattering blue and white broad-striped pyjama top, holding a diaper between their legs? Each time I watch the video I wish I wore something different, but at the time, it didn't matter.

The late nineties were pretty much pre-social media. While Vimeo and YouTube are now filled with live birth videos, back then it was much harder to find birth images, let alone a queer home birth with an eleven-person birth team. So, I would conclude, again and again, that it was worth the embarrassment to provide an alternative to the heterosexual, overly dramatic and often sensationalized images of birth then available in popular culture.

Video highlights: early labour, when the midwives arrive as I sit on the toilet having a contraction; the first internal exam where I am appalled to learn I am only two centimetres dilated; the birth team having a snack while being introduced on camera by Lois; me having contractions in a rocking chair, on the couch, in the hallway, on the bed; me, Lois and others walking up and down the hallway waiting for contractions during transition; people feeding me spoonfuls of honey and yogurt and gulps of Gatorade to keep my electrolytes up; the midwives checking the baby's heartbeat many times; my cousin holding my leg up as I push and sleep between contractions; people gathering around the bed for the birth; close-ups of my crotch as Sadie's head appears and then disappears, several times; the midwives encouraging me to look in the mirror at Sadie's head crowning; a final shot of Sadie's pre-birth head, looking like the earth, firmly lodged and making a perfect circle in the opening of my vagina; Kathie, at the beginning of a cold, sneezing as she gently supports my vagina to let Sadie's head out; the final contraction, the final push and a vernix-covered Sadie entering the world; my cousins, the cooks, offering me beer and cheesecake (my pre-ordered, post-birth refreshments), followed by chicken and vegetables; Sadie, in her tiny purple- and black-striped hat, latching on for the first time; everyone gathered around the bed, moved and slightly high from the miracle of birth.

For the most part, DPT participants were appreciative of the video. Though of course there was some cringing and nausea, people welcomed and learned from the opportunity to see birth up close, and to be let into this intimate moment in my life.

Now, twenty-six years later, I have watched my daughter being born countless times. I still get teary every time she comes out, but I am also fascinated by the video itself. What began as a home video of my labour and Sadie's birth is also a representation of home birth and the work of midwives before regulation, a glimpse into a sliver of Toronto lesbian life in the nineties and a celebration of queer community, as well as a learning tool about the stages of labour and labour support. The video is marked by a lack of self-consciousness. With the exception of one segment, in which Lois introduces the birth team to the camera, the people present, including myself, are so taken up with the process of labour and birth that the camera becomes inconsequential. The video captures the intimacy and the dynamics of twelve hours of our lives. But, like any documented version of a story, the narrative is incomplete and partial. I am struck by what is visible in the video, but even more so by what is not.

I got pregnant in 1991 with the assistance of a sperm bank and a fertility clinic. We consulted a fertility doctor about my irregular periods, and he suggested that if we found our own sperm donor, he would happily provide cycle monitoring and then send us home to inseminate in the old-fashioned lesbian way (with a turkey baster or, more practically, a syringe — without the needle).

But, alas, that known donor did not materialize, so we made the decision to choose a sperm donor from the catalogue and do cycle monitoring and insemination at the clinic.

Those who have had the fertility clinic experience are familiar with the routine of the early rise, the (in my case) bike ride to the clinic, the waiting room filled with parent wannabes and the long daily waits for blood tests and ultrasounds. The hope that you will be pricked by the practitioner who hurts their patients the least, that the follicles on the ultrasound screen will produce fertile eggs and, of course, that the insemination will result in a pregnancy. In my case, given that I did not ovulate until Day 54 of my cycle (Day 14 is average), I was there for many mornings.

I embraced the morning bike ride and immersed myself in a book while I waited at the clinic. I was grateful for the technology that could pinpoint my ovulation, and when I was shown the swelling follicles on the ultrasound, I felt almost pregnant. When I did actually get pregnant on my second try, despite a (probably inaccurate) diagnosis of polycystic ovarian syndrome, I was ecstatic. Of course, I did have to stand firm against the doctor's suggestion, after the first insemination attempt, that I take Clomid (a first-line fertility drug that, among other side effects, increases one's chances of multiple births) to make things simpler for everyone. And, as I lay spread-eagle in the stirrups awaiting insemination, he told me, "We've had others like you in our clinic." I was not sure exactly what he meant. Queer women? Single women? Women over thirty-five? Jews? Women with hairy legs?

I loved being pregnant. I have never before or since loved food as much as I did during those forty weeks, and I had a healthy, energetic and, for the most part, happy pregnancy. When it came time to give birth, I knew I wanted to do it at home. A week before my due date, I developed a severe infection in my baby finger and had to visit a hospital to have the fingernail removed. Sitting on a stretcher, surrounded by the sights, sounds and smells of the hospital, confirmed my decision. However, the video doesn't show the pressure I received from various quarters when I made the decision to give birth outside of a medical setting. Midwifery wasn't yet regulated in Canada in 1992; back then, a decision to birth at home was viewed by many as putting oneself and one's baby at undue risk. But I was clear what I wanted and confident in the skills and training of my midwives.

Of course, deciding to birth at home opened the door to more decisions — not the least of which is, who should be there? The video doesn't capture the pre-birth deliberations about who should attend. As I imagined being in labour and those I wanted present, the numbers kept growing. In the end, the room was filled with thirteen people, including the yet-to-be-born baby, two midwives and me. In true dyke fashion, we held a pre-birth potluck and get-together to talk about everything, take pictures and assign roles. At least one birth team member thought I was completely out of my mind.

The video also doesn't show the process of getting me into labour. The whole thing started as I was standing over the photocopier at Women's Press, where my partner worked at the time, photocopying an early version of what later became the Dykes Planning Tykes information kit. As the manual came off the photocopier, I felt a dribble down my leg and we figured we better *Call the Midwife*! The midwife wasn't sure if my water had broken, but I started to have mild contractions, or what I came to know as mild once I had experienced the more intense variety. I was told that if I didn't get into labour soon, I risked infection and a hospital birth, so I spent the next two days attempting to bring on labour. People took me for walks, I jumped up and down and imbibed homeopathics with labour-inducing properties. In the end, it was a castor oil–smoothie that first made me barf, and then brought on labour. The contractions started in earnest in the mid-afternoon.

Early labour was about figuring out how to approach this particular form of pain that was like nothing I had ever experienced. Someone had suggested that eye contact can be helpful to get through contractions. Lois and I tried this, but it was not helpful. We looked like actors in a bad porn movie as we looked into each other's eyes, with me moaning. This section of the video was cut. What ended up working for me was to hang on to another human body for every contraction.

My labour was long, but consistent and smooth. I learned to relax into the contractions. In fact, all my energy went into relaxing, a funny juxtaposition of concepts. I focused on my shoulders and on letting them go while I held onto another person each time my uterus contracted. While Lois was this person much of the time, I had my moments with every member of the birth team — downstairs, upstairs, sitting down, standing up, walking, on the toilet. I was in transition late at night, and the video shows me standing in the eerily quiet upstairs hall, holding onto a friend who is, sweetly, wearing a mother earth T-shirt. The support was physical, tangible and silent except for the moans, which were part of my relaxation strategy. My labour team held me for every contraction, but also rubbed my back, rubbed each other's backs, held my hand, timed contractions, took pictures, answered the phone and kept me nourished, even when I looked like I was going to regurgitate everything. As someone who can, at times, feel alone and unloved, or worse, unlovable, it is striking for me to witness how much love was in the house that night.

The video can't completely capture how the entire birth team fell into the rhythm of my labour. At one point, a couple of people left to pick up blankets and pillows for those who wanted to sleep. They said that even when they left the house, the car ride was marked by the rhythm of contractions. And when it came time for the final contraction, the midwives instructed me to pant to prevent tearing. In the video, you can hear the whole room panting with me as Sadie enters the world.

For me, labour and birth took place in a liminal space, moments and hours outside of time and place. And yet despite the profundity and exquisiteness of the process, interpersonal dynamics did not cease. In the video we don't see my partner in the backyard being talked down from feeling that her place as my primary support was being usurped by another member of the birth team.

We're not aware of another birth team member's concerns that being present at this event will trigger her childhood sexual abuse, or another's worries that my becoming a parent will detract from my ability to be present for her as a friend.

My labour and the birth of our daughter did not transform the relationship between Lois and me. There is a vulnerability for me in the existence of this video, because those who watch it see me and Lois at the intimate moment of our daughter's birth. How do they see us? As we walk up and down the hall, late at night, me in my pyjama top and diaper, waiting for contractions that come at the same place each time, I recall the comfort I derived from Lois's body and steadiness. I see us talking quietly into each other's ears, me telling her what is going on and what I need, us joking about when the contractions will come and stopping our conversation when I am taken over by a contraction and need to hold onto her. We are connected.

But I also see moments of disconnection, moments when I think I see, or perhaps I only recall, the small tightenings of my face and stomach as I react to some of her words and behaviours — those niggling things that bug you in a close relationship. And as I watch these moments, over and over, each time the video is shown, I see how my reactions are more about me than her. I am afraid, even when giving birth, surrounded by an eleven-member birth team entirely focused on my body and its needs and on loving me, that I will be abandoned. I struggle to hold onto the fact that I am loved and held, even when I am actively being loved and physically held.

Being in labour was all about the breath — breathing into every contraction with the intention of relaxing. In the video, as I enter the space between contractions, I look almost drugged. But my recollection is of a heightened awareness of everything going on in the room. I know that labour produces a particular kind of endorphin that provides natural pain relief. What seemed unmanageable at two centimetres somehow became manageable as my labour progressed — something kicks in that makes it possible to endure contraction after contraction, hour after hour. Being in labour put me in the present moment like nothing before or since. Ironically, that in-the-moment experience was captured on video and the video has become the story. What would I recall of the experience if the video did not exist? What story would we tell of Sadie's birth?

There is something frightening about childbirth, the way the body opens to let out a whole human head, followed by a body. When Sadie watched the video for the first time, she asked, with some concern, "But how does it close up?" Big heads run in my family, and I worried about this. In the end, it was not only her head, but also her arms positioned beside her ears that I had to push out. It felt like shitting a watermelon. During those final contractions, the midwives offer me a mirror several times as encouragement, so I can see the progress I am making. The video shows me looking at the mirror half-heartedly, as if doing them a favour. It was too much effort at that point; all my energy had to go to pushing that baby out. Team members gasp when her head crowns: the excitement that she is about to be born is palpable. I, on the other hand, am singularly concerned with getting the baby out of my body. I am so tired that I am sleeping between contractions. My partner is massaging my nipples to bring on contractions, one midwife is detecting the next contraction by placing her hand at the top of my gigantic belly, the second midwife is monitoring the baby's heartbeat with a stethoscope, my cousin is holding my leg on her shoulder, Amy is videotaping and taking photos, and Mo brings a ringing telephone into the room. My dad hears his granddaughter being born from an airport in Hawaii. "It sounds like a football match," he says, referring to the cheers that erupt when Sadie makes her entrance.

Sadie was born at 5 a.m. on April 24, 1992. When morning broke it was sunny outside — one of the first warm, sunny days after a gruelling and interminably long Toronto winter. The final shots in the edited version of the video are of Sadie nursing and my friend handing me a beer. I'm told I can take only a few sips for fear of bleeding from a tired uterus. I take a swig and, as if in a beer commercial, announce, "After a long day's work ..." Nothing like a cold beer. At that moment there was nothing better than lying in bed with my newborn baby on me, Lois behind me, a gaggle of loving lesbians surrounding me and taking a swig of cold beer. I recall the shadows of the sun in our bedroom and the sense that things could not have been more perfect.

Following the birth, I was high for days. The midwives told us that Sadie, tired from the act of being born, would soon have a long sleep. They advised me that when that happens, I should sleep, too. In fact, it never happened — I am still waiting for Sadie to have her long sleep. At the time, however, it was irrelevant; I couldn't have slept anyway, as I was too ecstatic about her arrival and about the process of bringing her into the world.

Those who attended the birth were high, too, but eventually they reluctantly left the cocoon we had created through the rhythms of labour and the spirit of community, friendship and love. They had to return to jobs, to housework, to meetings, to life. As they walked out into the sunshine that day, none of us knew what was to come. Lois and I separated when Sadie was ten years old. Though not without its challenges, we remain solid co-parents and tight friends. Some of the people who attended the birth became other parents to Sadie; others are no longer in our lives. Some have become parents themselves, through birth or adoption. One of the midwives is no longer a midwife. We couldn't know any of this at the time. All we knew was that we had all been part of a baby being born. And we have the video to prove it.

Nursing My Way to Motherhood

Katie Taylor

I stood behind my wife, pressing my hands into the sides of her hips to relieve the pressure, as our son made his slow descent down her birth canal. In the quiet moment before the next contraction, the sound of my breast pump filled the room. We looked at our own reflections in the windows spanning the wall, the lights of Burlington, Vermont, blinking back at us.

My wife closed her eyes and let out a soft moan of pain. I manoeuvred my arms around the tubes that connected my breasts to the machine, put my hands onto her hips and pressed.

I got pregnant the first time we tried. It was with an intrauterine insemination (IUI) at our doctor's office. We'd discussed the turkey baster method, but sperm was expensive, I was getting older every day and I had a suspicion something in my reproductive system wasn't on the up and up. So, we ran toward medical intervention with our arms wide open.

My wife brought home pizza and Martinelli's. I took a photo of the digital pee test that shouted "Pregnant," called my mom and my sister to share the news and started a secret baby-focused Pinterest page.

The spotting started almost immediately. I whispered to the tiny little bundle of cells in my uterus, "It's safe for you in there. Please stay."

The nurse called on Memorial Day. The blood tests showed dropping hormone levels, a sign of a nonviable pregnancy. I stood on the slate tiles in the entryway of our new home, the one with the perfect little room for a nursery, and cried onto my wife's shoulder.

I don't envy doctors or nurses. I've never had to break someone's heart as part of my job.

We waited three months before trying again, still hopeful. Yet month after month, the tests came back negative. Three years later, after an in vitro fertilization (IVF), a miscarriage and too many tears, we made a new plan: I would start the IVF process again, and my wife would start getting IUIs. Whoever got pregnant first was having our baby.

I resisted the idea of shared nursing. My body had firmly refused to get or stay pregnant. Mothering was clearly not in its lexicon. Perhaps it was time I got the message.

Besides, I told my wife, after she had done the work of carrying a baby around for nine months and then pushing it out with the strength of her own body, she deserved the bond of breastfeeding. I did not.

"But you tried for years. Of course you deserve it," she argued. "And anyway, I want the help."

We'd talked to so many of our female friends in hetero relationships who felt overwhelmed by breastfeeding. Having someone to take a few of the middle-of-the-night nursing sessions? *Sign me up.*

I recognized that I would not have been so sharing. As wrapped up as I was in the shame of infertility and the insatiable desire to create life, I knew I would have held tightly to that connection between mother and baby. But my wife was either more generous or more afraid of being solely responsible for the sustenance of a tiny human being. Or both.

So, we agreed I would try.

I started pumping six weeks before the due date, following a protocol I'd found online for inducing lactation. I never could quite manage the recommended eight times a day; the demands of work and the seduction of sleep capped me at seven. I read chick lit as

I pumped. A city girl running from a failed affair fell in love with a shy country boy while I winced through the early pain, when nothing but air filled the bottles. In the days right before our son was born, I read about a French bookstore owner on a journey to find his last love while drops of milk fell from my nipples.

Inducing lactation requires three things: starting birth control six months before the baby is due, taking a medication called Domperidone for six months before and throughout breastfeeding, and then stopping birth control and pumping every three hours for the six weeks leading up to the due date.

Domperidone, a gastrointestinal medication that can cause lactation as a side effect, is not approved for sale in the US. Though it is available for sale in most other countries, the U.S. Food and Drug Administration banned it in 2004 because of cardiac impacts in severely ill patients who were given the drug intravenously.

A rule-follower by nature, I had some apprehension about acquiring the drug. Through a Facebook group for queer nongestational parents, I'd learned where to order it online and been assured that placing the order for a specific different product would result in Domperidone showing up on my doorstep. I imagined a SWAT team arriving alongside it, guns extended as they grabbed the packages and brought me in for questioning.

I visited my doctor, hopeful that she'd agree the ban was unreasonable and prescribe it anyway. Yet after weighing my ability to breastfeed against her medical licence, she didn't accommodate.

"There are herbs you can take," she told me. "And start the pumping routine as soon as possible. It may work. It may not. Think of it as an experiment."

"An experiment?" I exclaimed later to my wife. "If I'm going to do all this, I want it to work. I want to be able to feed our son. I don't want an experiment."

I called a local lactation consultant who said exactly what I wanted to hear — the ban on the drug in its pill form was irrational; she recommended Domperidone to lots of mothers with low milk supply and I should absolutely go for it. I placed my order that night.

I was sitting at my desk the next day when my cellphone rang from a number I didn't recognize. On the other end of the scratchy line, a woman yelled at me, "Tell your bank approve charge. You place order. Bank not approve. You tell them approve. We do it again."

My hands shook as I hung up. I was sure that I had just provided our credit card information to a scam operation, that our identities were being stolen by someone in a foreign country at that very moment. Perhaps I was too anxious for induced lactation.

Then I thought of a tiny baby snuggled against my body, being comforted by my milk.

I called the credit card company. "Yeah, you've got two charges here for $138.10. One's for electronics and one's for clothing," the man said.

I scrambled for how to respond. The whole thing sounded wildly suspicious to me. I thought it must to the man on the phone, too. After he hung up, he would probably call the authorities to let them know about the shady international transactions. I told him I wanted the charge to go through. "Clothing or electronics?" he asked. "Or both?"

"Um," I hesitated. "Electronics?"

The charge went through and a month later a rubber-banded bundle of blister packs with little yellow pills showed up in my mailbox.

Afterwards, I discovered a Canadian seller with slightly less intrigue, and the pills arrived faster and still in the original boxes, providing me a bit more peace of mind.

"I know this appointment is supposed to be about you," my wife's obstetrician-gynaecologist said at one of her monthly visits. "But," and she turned toward me, her eyes lit with excitement, "I really want to hear about this."

I explained the birth control and the pumping and the shady Domperidone purchases.

"And? Are you getting any milk?"

When I told her I was pumping between one and two ounces at every pumping session, her eyes got big. "Well, that's enough to feed a newborn!"

The interest continued at the hospital. I assumed that since we were in Burlington, where lesbians abound, the doctors and nurses would have encountered a lesbian non-gestational parent who was breastfeeding, but I was wrong.

After our son was born, nurses entered our room and made straight for me as I held an impossibly tiny little creature up to my breast. They peered closely, making suggestions for how to hold the baby and what to look for to make sure he was drinking. I suspected they all secretly wanted to see for themselves.

I felt like a science experiment — but the good kind, where the volcano shoots higher than anyone expected.

We sat in the nursery in the middle of the night, the lights turned down low as I rocked back and forth in our padded glider, a squishy, swaddled baby nestled in the crook of my arm, his eyes closed as he suckled at my breast. I closed my own eyes and let my head rest against the back of the chair, drifting in and out of sleep as I fed this child I had not given birth to, who shared not a scrap of my DNA but who was so clearly mine. Across from me, my wife sat in a grey metal folding chair, the plastic bottles attached to her breasts slowly filling with butter-coloured milk. Three hours later, we'd sit in opposite positions, the extra sleep we thought we'd get from being able to share the load hampered by breasts that demanded emptying regardless of our plans.

In the beginning, we were interchangeable. A boob was a boob was a boob. Latching was not quite as easy with my wife, but she developed a system with our son as they spent their days together those first three months. When I got home, he was happy to switch things up and nurse from me until bedtime.

Eventually he developed preferences. Once my wife went back to work, we tried to change the routine and have her feed him in the evenings. Before bed, he would cry and push against her with all the force his little body could muster. I went into the other room, tried to disappear, be silent so that he wouldn't know I was there.

"He wants you," she would say with a clenched jaw and tears in her eyes as she handed him over.

"I'm so sorry," I'd whisper.

We talked to the doctor, our lactation consultant, a different lactation consultant, other co-nursing moms on a Facebook group — no one knew how to cure him of preference. I cringed as the doctor told us that babies often identify one parent as the "comfort" parent. I glanced over at my wife, who had a similarly pained expression on her face. "Not that the other parent is chopped liver," the doctor hedged. "They're just usually the fun one. Besides, this won't be the last time what he wants and what you want conflict. This is good training for the future."

Throughout my wife's pregnancy, I'd been stung by friends or acquaintances who congratulated only my wife, looked only at her when speaking about the baby or our future as parents. Her growing belly was a constant physical reminder that she would be forever connected to our child in a way I never could be, and the comments of others seemed to broadcast my deep fear: that I was irrelevant in all this.

In the weeks before our son was born, I should have been afraid of the sleepless nights and the constant decision-making, but instead I obsessed over whether people would see me as his mother, whether he would, whether I would.

In the hospital a few hours after my wife gave birth, the nurses prepared to move us from Labour and Delivery to the Mother-Baby Unit. It was two or three in the morning, and the unit was full. They were going to have to put us in one of the shared rooms. For safety reasons, the nurse told me apologetically, only the mother and baby could stay in the room overnight.

I looked at her, my mouth agape. My son was mere hours old and I was going to have to be separated from him. And from my wife, who had just done the hardest thing I'd ever seen and would have to spend the rest of the night without me.

"Is there any way …?" I asked, letting the question trail off. I couldn't wrap my head around what they were saying.

"I'm not comfortable with that," my wife said.

"Well," the nurse said, scrunching up her forehead in thought. "You are breastfeeding." My son was, in fact, attempting to attach himself to my breast at that moment. "Let me see what I can do," she said as she left the room.

As she walked us to the new unit, the nurse told me, rather conspiratorially, that partners are not normally allowed to stay in shared rooms overnight, but she'd told them I needed to stay because I was also feeding our newborn baby. "There's only a chair for you to sleep in," she told me.

"Not a problem," I assured her. "Thank you."

I hated to think of the fathers and mothers sent away in the first hours of their babies' lives. Sitting in that chair next to my wife's bed, watching my son's tiny chest rising and falling, I saw that breastfeeding made me a mother in other people's eyes, whether I birthed him or not.

The truth is this: I became his mother the moment I saw the faint pink line on the pregnancy test. I was his mother while I massaged my pregnant wife's swollen calves each night, and I was his mother when my alarm went off at 4 a.m. and I shuffled to the sofa and pulled out my pump. I was always his mother, but breastfeeding created a tangible way for me — and others — to see my place in our new little family.

It's 6:45 p.m., and my wife and I sit next to each other on the grey couch in our living room, my arm slung around her shoulder. Our son has taken to nursing sitting up, a position that allows him to turn his head to the side and look at what's going on around him. He does this now, his mouth clasped onto my wife's breast while he watches me.

He pulls off and reaches his arms out toward me, and I grab his chunky little body and slide him over to sit on my lap, him grasping at my breast as I pull it out of my bra. He latches on and turns his head to the side, watching my wife with his big blue eyes. She puts her arm around my shoulder and snuggles in close to us.

"This is nice," she says.

I nod and kiss her on the forehead.

It's perfect.

IT'S NORMAL NOT TO KNOW

Heather Osborne

"I have a daddy?" my son, L, asked me casually as we flipped through board books in the library.

Like more than a few questions that a two-year-old can come up with, this one seemed to wander in from nowhere in particular. Up until a moment ago, L had been busy admiring one of his favourite sorts of constructions: a line. In this case, it was a line of every toddler-sized chair appropriated from the library's snack area. Fifteen or more red, yellow and purple plastic chairs in a row provided L with much aesthetic pleasure and me with a vague sense of guilt, wondering about fire codes. Still, the librarians hadn't complained, and I knew better than to get between this boy and his line.

I knew better than to deflect his question about daddies, too. L recently had an epiphany: he discovered *frustration*. While he hadn't yet connected my occasional exasperation with his lengthy series of "But why?" interrogations, he could pinpoint my mood with disarming accuracy. And it didn't slow his questions in the least. "Mama, why you say 'ugh?' Mama, you frustrated?"

Besides, I'd been anticipating the daddy question since long before L was even born. It was certainly the number one question my wife, Beth, and I were asked when the topic of L's conception came up. But for that very reason, Beth and I had been planning for this day, though perhaps I hadn't expected it so soon. "No," I said with equal, if feigned, ease. "You don't have a daddy. You have a Mommy and a Mama."

"You're my mama!" he exclaimed, his face lighting up. He loved to guess the answers to questions. When Beth and I spoke in the third person around him — *I think someone around here needs a bath* — L was always incredibly proud of himself for breaking the code. "That's me!" he'd say, delighted. "*I* need a bath!"

"That's right, I'm your mama," I said. I could have left it there, but I thought L might need a little more reinforcement than most kids about what families look like. "Some families have a mommy and a mama, some have two daddies and some have a mommy and a daddy."

I considered this a pretty good speech, but L had already moved on. "I can have a snack?" he asked next. We got out the container of Goldfish crackers and debated how many crackers were too many, considering it was an hour before dinner. L, true to two-year-old form, had much stronger opinions on Goldfish than about either genetics or parenting.

When Beth and I decided to have a baby, one of the hoops the fertility clinic asked us to jump through — a hoop, like most of them, designed with the straight couple in mind — had been a visit with a psychologist. She ushered us into her office and patted us into chairs. Boxes of Kleenex dotted the shelves around us. I wondered about the couples who'd been here before — what uncomfortable, unspoken resentments or heart-squeezing fears they might have to confess. The psychologist gazed at us sincerely, and gently asked if we'd be comfortable raising a child conceived with a stranger's DNA.

Beth and I glanced sidelong at each other. "Well, yeah?" I said, refraining from too overt a *duh*.

"How else would we do it?" Beth chimed in. We'd talked about it, done the research. We'd already made the choice of an open donation, rather than closing off our potential child from the donor if she or he decided to learn more about her or his biological roots. We preferred a stranger to the more challenging intimacy of a known donor. Though we were paying three hundred dollars an hour for the psychologist's sign-off, and aware of the irony that we were being held to higher standards than most parents, we felt happy, eager. All we needed was a little boost — an assist, if you will, to get the puck in the net. The puck's bona fides weren't as important as scoring the goal.

The psychologist smiled, though she seemed hesitant to be happy for us quite yet. "Well, but what will you tell your child, when he asks about where he came from?"

"That he had a donor?" I suggested, wondering if the question was a trap.

The psychologist beamed. "Yes. Yes, we do recommend that. We like to call the donor a 'helper' rather than a father."

"That makes sense," Beth said, nodding as earnestly as the psychologist — trying, I thought, to make the psychologist comfortable with our comfort. We all nodded to each other. Beth squeezed my hand. I grinned sappily at her. We turned to the psychologist to field her next question.

Our one-hour appointment concluded in twenty minutes. We still paid the three hundred dollars.

Our fertility doctor's resident was the first to admit that many of the tests the clinic required were probably unnecessary in our case. There was no evidence, however specious, that my fallopian tubes weren't the Splash Mountain of egg cells, each one gleefully shooting down the pipeline at a well-charted twenty-seven-day interval. Nevertheless, I was apologetically directed to the local hospital to have dye squirted up where no dye should ever go. "Just to see if there are any blockages," the resident said, before confessing with a wince, "this is probably the worst one."

She was right: no pap smear, nor even childbirth, compares in my memory to being slapped down, pried open, spurted full of dye and encouraged to roll around until it foamed out where it should. My personal northwest passage was well and truly open to travellers, but I clenched my teeth and whimpered through the excruciating minutes while a brusque Nurse Franklin went exploring. "This isn't that bad," she insisted. "Haven't you had sex before?"

"Never with a *man*," I spat vengefully, finally allowed to roll clear of the speculum.

A bemused "Oh" was the full extent of any apology I received. Still, my experience proved one thing: I found that I could disarm questioners with forthright good humour. "Yes, we bought the sperm online. Just like browsing on Amazon!"

Reactions to this varied from hesitation to authentic interest. Most people of my acquaintance were happy to share in my biology geekery. "Cool!" they'd say. "Hair? Eyes? Height?"

"Checkboxes for all of them," I boasted. "It turns out it's cheaper if you buy in bulk."

I knew I was lucky to have such an assortment of donors to choose from. I was determined to pick someone who reminded me of Beth: an oval face with a pointed chin, dark blond hair and blue eyes.

"You can't be sure the baby will have blue eyes," Beth pointed out. She was more interested in perusing the donors' personal essays for evidence of emotional stability. Once I'd narrowed down the selection to guys whose cheekbones matched hers, she made the final selection. "He seems kind," she said, "and he likes cats." Sold.

My eyes are a medium brown. I'd drawn enough high school Punnett squares to know there was a likelihood the donor's blue allele would be overwritten. But there was a chance: my father's eyes were blue, and so were all my siblings'. Any way you sliced it, I had a recessive blue hiding in my DNA. I was confident that I'd beat the coin toss.

L was born with indigo eyes that lightened to a bright, happy blue. Strangers have chuckled over him, then told Beth his face is just like his mom's. Even people who know how we conceived have pointed out a likeness. "It's not weird to say, is it? He really does look like her!"

I've always been as proud as if I'd sorted the chromosomes myself.

After the question of the semen's provenance (my mother's only hand-wringing over our choices concerned whether the gentleman in question could be proven to have a professional degree), the next most common concern we encountered was, "But which one of you will be the mom?"

Beth and I funded the fertility treatment with a bequest from my grandmother. I never got a chance to ask if she approved of how I spent my inheritance. She could be crusty, with a sardonic, cut-the-bullshit stare. If I'd had a chance to tell her I was pregnant, I'm sure she wouldn't have hesitated to ask the same question that seemed to plague most people when they found out what we intended: What will the baby *call* you?

It helped that we knew a few other lesbian couples who'd grappled with the same question. Mommy and Mama were strong contenders from the beginning.

"Since I call my mother Mom," I said, "I think it'd be easier to call you Mom. So I'll be Mama."

"I couldn't call you Mom," Beth said, "because that's what I call *my* mother. So I'll be Mom."

Not unusually, we'd come at the problem with the same logic, and ended up with a complementary solution. All it took after that was nine months of practice, while we talked to L through my belly.

By now, our names are so engrained that L has definite expectations about who is who. Recently he spent the day with my brother and his three cousins. When I came to collect him, he was happy to see me, but he kept looking around for Beth. "Where's Mommy?" he asked.

"She's not coming," I said. "She's at work."

"But my uncle said Mommy coming to pick me up!"

I laughed. "Sounds like your uncle made a mistake."

L loved hearing that a grown-up had been mistaken. "That's so silly!"

"Yup, he's pretty silly sometimes. So, do you want soup or sandwiches for dinner?"

I wasn't too worried about my brother's slip. Familiar words rise quicker to the tongue. The distinction might seem artificial:

in the plural, Beth and I are collectively moms. My family doesn't mean to be dismissive by getting it wrong. It can sometimes feel like they haven't been paying attention, but I've had to put in the same work, and I still make the same mistake. I told the story of L's confusion to my brother, like a joke. He's an easygoing person, and he accepted the implicit correction with a laugh.

I can't resent anyone for calling me Mom, even if I've corrected them before. Early in my pregnancy, Beth floated the idea of being Daddy rather than Mom. After all, she's Uncle Beth to our nephews. My brother and sister-in-law call her Uncle Beth when speaking of her to their boys. When my oldest nephew was two, he'd cheerfully yell "Unca B!" whenever he saw her.

Yet I didn't grapple well with the suggestion. I wavered, shrugged. "I don't know ..."

In retrospect, my hesitation feels like a failure. I wasn't as open as I should have been. It would have been a struggle to consistently remember to say Daddy. I might have been embarrassed to explain the choice to people who asked — another weakness. Maybe I underestimated Beth's desire to be a daddy. But she saw my discomfort and accepted it. So, while I will correct people when they forget that I'm L's Mama, I won't resent them for it.

L knows that some children have daddies. He started at a preschool when he turned one. By two, he could point out all his classmates' parents. "That's my friend's daddy!" he'd say. Or, "Aaron's daddy picks him up."

Daddies exist in his world. They are real creatures, though somewhat ill-defined. The fact that L doesn't have one simply doesn't bother him.

One morning, a girl in his class happened to call her mother Mama in L's hearing.

"Is that her Mommy?" he asked me, kicking his feet while I struggled to change his boots for indoor shoes.

"Yes," I said, distracted. "Other foot."

L laughed, "But she call her Mama! That's her Mommy!"

"Maybe she doesn't have a Mama," I said, belatedly catching up to L's point. "Maybe she calls her Mommy Mama sometimes."

"No!" L said, drawing out the word and scrunching up his nose at me like I'd told a joke. Like his uncle, his friend had made a silly mistake. She must have a Mama somewhere — after all, daddies might be imaginary, but mamas and mommies simply weren't interchangeable.

At the library, I paged through the board book L had chosen, *Uh-Oh!* by Shutta Crum and Patrice Barton. The illustrations showed a boy and a mother with brown hair, and a girl and a mother with blond hair. Crum and Barton probably intended to show two families enjoying the beach together, but I happily repurposed the story as a Mommy, a Mama, and their two children. L loved it.

It wasn't the first time I'd read a book to L and made an editorial decision to replace the Daddy with a Mama. Other than *Mommy, Mama, and Me* by Leslea Newman, which was given to us as a baby shower gift from a friend — a lesbian and a children's librarian, an excellent combination — there just weren't that many books that showed families like ours. I wasn't against daddies in books by any means, but when the characters are cartoon bears, it's easy enough to replace the word Daddy on the fly.

But L is now getting started on the idea of gender. I'm careful to avoid absolutes with him when I discuss it. "Most women don't have penises," I told him, while he examined a naked Barbie doll of uncertain origin and asked about her smooth plastic crotch.

"I have a penis," he pointed out.

"Well, you're probably not a woman," I said. "You're a boy, and usually boys have penises."

"You a woman?" he asked, with much the same casual curiosity he'd shown about daddies.

"Yes," I said.

"And Mommy a woman!" he exclaimed. With that, his questions ended; he'd filed away the important answers. Barbie was discarded in favour of his beloved wooden train.

Someday, L will learn to read and realize just how many daddies populate his books. Someday, he might wonder about where babies come from, and refuse to be distracted by Goldfish crackers — as hard as that is to imagine now.

Still, he has a Mommy and a Mama who love him. We've laid the foundation, and I hope that when his questions come, he'll be more than ready for the answers.

LOVING BENJAMIN

Gail Marlene Schwartz

PART FIVE: BEGINNING

His eyes are dark and warm, like hot chocolate, and his movements are punctuated and full of life, like a baby Charlie Chaplin. His new lips feel strangely capable on my nipple.

His gaze meets mine and I whisper, "Well hello, Benjamin," my voice grainy from the surgery.

I nurse him hello and I nurse him goodbye. I haven't seen him since.

PART ONE: ANOTHER BEGINNING

"Congratulations!"

I listen to the message three times to make sure it's real. Finally, I drop the phone and bolt out the door, barefooted, running to find Lucie, who is walking the dog, shouting, "We're pregnant! We're pregnant!!!"

PART TWO: WAITING AND WEIGHING

Our first ultrasound happens at eight weeks. The technician rubs jelly on my belly and a tiny pulsing heart appears on the screen.

And then, another.

Two bodies. Two heartbeats.

At home that evening, we celebrate with flowers: two yellow mums for them, a white for Lucie and a purple for me. We light candles, hold hands, weep for joy.

I step on the scale. 161 pounds. No gain yet.

Our doctor gives me screening tests at week twelve. Afterwards she sits us down; she's concerned about the nuchal translucency scan, which indicates that Baby B has a one-in-three chance of having Down Syndrome. She strongly recommends an early amniocentesis, which would be definitive. "I could do it tomorrow," she says. Ninety-five percent of women who get this news choose abortion, she tells us, and if it's necessary, sooner is better for the healthy twin.

I am numb and cannot speak.

We schedule an appointment for the amniocentesis in a few days to give ourselves time to think. I cry silently in the car going home, wiping my cheeks and nose with the grey fleece of my jacket.

During the next few days, I think about my fantasy children. One girl and one boy. Talented. Smart. Musician and cartoonist. Successful. People who other people cherish. People who care for the world and make me proud.

Of course, neither of those children has Down Syndrome.

Retarded. Slow. Special needs. Mentally handicapped.

Somebody whom 95 percent of people choose to abort.

No, this news does not fit into my plans at all.

Suddenly I am deeply ashamed. I want to tuck myself into the corner, under the loose floorboard in our bedroom, where nobody can see me.

Lucie and I talk for hours. We already feel like parents and realize that abortion is not an option for us. Our research tells us that Down Syndrome babies are easily adoptable by families who feel called to raise special needs kids.

I step on the scale. Again and again and again.

165.

165.

168.

My brain does somersaults around the one-in-three odds. Sixty-six percent of the people who get this news have normal kids, I reason. Medical doctors are such alarmists. Two out of three, two out of three, two out of three.

I see a new mom pushing her twins in a double stroller down the street. I turn around and cover four extra blocks to avoid her.

171.

172.

174.

It's Halloween. We spend hours on our costumes. Lucie is a witch and I am the Headless Horseman. We make an orange-themed dinner for friends: sweet potato fries, pumpkin soup, cheese puffs. We light candles and carve intricate designs into pumpkins à la Martha Stewart.

172.

175.

175.

I feel my capacity for closeness shut down, like a trap door, and I sink deeper and deeper into the darkness. I stop returning phone calls and start going back to bed after breakfast. Sometimes I stay there until lunch.

I think of my own mother, just twenty-two at my birth. An unplanned pregnancy, I wasn't the child she had imagined, either: a beautiful, feminine girl who would play quietly with dolls, do as she's told, and take good care of Mommy.

Daily life with her was terrifying.

What if she had given me up?

175.

176.

175.

PART THREE: MOVING THROUGH THE MIDDLE

The doctor calls two weeks later with the results of the amniocentesis. Baby B has Down Syndrome.

The waiting is over.

I spend the day with Lucie. We cry and hold each other as we wander around the house. I look for something to fill myself with: flax toast with peanut butter, semi-sweet chocolate morsels,

Lucky Charms cereal with rice milk, a Granny Smith apple and some cheddar.

The gaping hole remains in the depths of my pregnant belly.

In the evening, I make the mistake of calling my mother. She listens silently for a moment before speaking. "You're not going to KEEP it, are you?" I hang up quietly and lie down on the couch and stay there, staring out the window, until morning.

Lucie and I talk at breakfast before she leaves for work. We know deep in our hearts that we cannot provide for Baby B. Our advancing ages and my career are reason enough; I don't even have to face my initial shame.

179.

177.

178.

I float out, further and further from my tribe. I am too broken to manage others' reactions, judgments, even their clumsy, kind offers of, "Is there anything I can do?"

179.

180.

180.

I spend more and more time in bed.

PART FOUR: (RE)BIRTH

Quietness. Emptiness. Agony.

My belly pushes out, more and more, and I sleep in short spurts. My maternity pants keep falling down and I can't walk to the corner without feeling breathless.

We find out they are two boys and decide to name them: Baby A is Alexi. Baby B is Benjamin. We use their hospital initials to honour their time as twins, kicking, elbowing and hiccupping inside me.

182.

183.

184.

Between week thirty-two and thirty-three, the adoption proceedings begin. We shed tears of relief to find out there is a family waiting for little Benjamin.

Repeated questions about us being sure of our decision are difficult.

We are sure ... and we are sad.

185.

187.

187.

Occasionally I am still overtaken by fear. "What if there's something wrong with Alexi?" "What if something happens at the birth?" "What if I am a terrible mother?"

Elbows and heels glide across my middle so I focus there. The fear retreats into the shadow of the miracle and starts loosening its grip on my soul.

190.

191.

192.

PART FIVE: BEGINNING, AGAIN

At thirty-six weeks, my doctor tells me I am having light contractions and that Benjamin's heart rate is dropping dangerously low with each one. She suggests going ahead with an induction, knowing how important a vaginal birth is to me. "We can always wheel you across the hall to the OR for a C-section if there's any problem."

I look at her, puzzled. "But couldn't Benjamin die quickly with stronger contractions?" She just looks at me, and finally shrugs. I realize then that my doctor is thinking only of Alexi. She is willing to sacrifice Benjamin, seeing him like most of the outside world will see him. My mind runs through all of the reasons C-sections are bad for babies; this is not how I want my son to enter the world. But at that moment, I am Benjamin's mother too, his birth mother, and my job is clear. I make the decision and the nurses begin prepping me for surgery.

I tell our doula, Leslie, and the hospital staff that I do not want to see Benjamin at all after the birth. I need to focus on Alexi and not get bogged down in grief.

Frightened and shivering, I am wheeled into the OR in my gown. I am given several medications in my spine and slowly sensations in my bottom half fade away. Lucie comes in after about fifteen minutes and holds my hand. At some points I am losing so much blood that nausea almost overcomes me. Finally, they pull Alexi out and I hear him wail. The nurse puts him on my chest for a few moments before whisking him away to be cleaned. They take Benjamin out next and quickly bring him elsewhere.

When we arrive in the recovery room, both babies are there. It seems the doctors had forgotten my request. A nurse takes Alexi away for some extra oxygen and Benjamin remains in his little plastic bassinet, quietly smacking his tiny lips together. Leslie comments casually that he wants to nurse. I throw caution to the wind, take him in my arms and give it my best effort: my first moment of breastfeeding. He latches on and nurses like a pro, all the while maintaining eye contact.

His eyes are dark and warm, like hot chocolate, and his movements are punctuated and full of life, like a baby Charlie Chaplin. His new lips feel strangely capable on my nipple.

His gaze meets mine and I whisper, "Well hello, Benjamin," my voice grainy from the surgery.

I nurse him hello and I nurse him goodbye. I haven't seen him since.

O-HESO (BELLY BUTTON)

Terrie Hamazaki

August 10, 2016, Vancouver, Canada
The square piece of bone-white goat rawhide is in my right hand. I'm
holding a lighter in my other hand, waiting for the timer on my phone
to signal 6:37 p.m., the exact moment of my birth fifty-five years ago
today. I'm sitting, facing east, on a log close to the shoreline of English
Bay. The grey sand on the beach is a flat surface into which variously
shaped shoe prints have scuffed up the appearance of moon craters. There
are half-hidden cigarette butts and tiny pebbles underneath my sneak-
ered feet. I breathe in and out slowly and focus on a puff of goose down
that's caught in the sand, its wispy tendrils fluttering in the slight sea
breeze. In the instant that my phone vibrates on the log beside me, I
strike the lighter and find its flame. I hold it to the skin, which blackens
on contact.

In 1995, I was excited to build a family with my partner. She was
the second woman I'd been involved with since coming out as
a lesbian in 1989 at the age of twenty-eight. We decided that I
would be the one to try to conceive by way of artificial insemination at the local fertility clinic. After a series of tests to determine
that I was in excellent reproductive health, we finally found ourselves seated in comfortable leather chairs in the clinic conference
room at our first appointment, perusing the thick binders of donor profiles. We quickly winnowed through the pile after reading
each man's essay on why they became a donor and learning about
their background: age, religion, ethnicity, medical history and education. It was important for us that the donor wished to remain
anonymous, unknown. The question of whether using an unknown
donor could impact on our child was a difficult one to consider,

but we had reasons for our choice. As the biological mother, my relationship to the baby was clear, but we believed that having a known donor could potentially usurp my partner's parental status, as she was not biologically related. As well, based on our individual experiences, we defined a father as merely a sperm donor; we could re-define it in our butch-femme lesbian family. The procedure was costly at four hundred dollars each treatment (the sperm was often acquired from the US), and we budgeted a set amount.

The process was sterile and uninspired. We brought with us a diaper bag filled with items such as a teddy bear, two binkies and an old fleece baby blanket of mine. We also carried in a portable cassette player and a collection of nursery rhymes tapes. I lay on the table, socked feet in stirrups, while the nurse prepared the insemination procedure. As my partner pushed down the syringe attached to the fine sperm-filled catheter that was inserted into my uterus, I closed my eyes, imagining ladybugs pulling rowboats under twinkling stars. We kissed deeply before and after the proceedings.

Over a two-year period, from 1998 to 2000 — despite my being labelled as high-risk due to my "advanced" age of thirty-six when I began inseminating — I tried a total of eight times. There were several early miscarriages and in December 1999 I had a third ectopic pregnancy. The medical staff had gently advised me about the possibility of a second ectopic after my first, and a third after my second. But I wasn't ready to surrender. I was still ovulating, producing eggs, wanting a child, yearning for motherhood. I had been pregnant once before when I was twenty-seven after a one-night stand of unprotected sex. And before I chose to terminate that pregnancy, I knew that my body could sustain another life. I trusted my body.

The third ectopic pregnancy nearly killed me. The dose of methotrexate I'd received at the clinic failed to stop the rapidly growing cells of the pregnancy, and it continued to grow until it burst through my left fallopian tube, spilling blood into my abdominal cavity. In the hospital emergency department, the nurses were unable to examine me using an ultrasound machine because

I'd wrapped my arms tightly around my mid-section that was cramped in agonizing pain. My body was going into shock and they struggled to find a vein in which to insert the IV. Three people tried and when one finally succeeded, I remember seeing through my half-closed eyes that they air high-fived. "Count backwards from one hundred," said a masculine voice. Then, a feminine voice yelling, "Get her in now! Go!"

When I awoke, I looked out the window of my shared room at whiteness. It had snowed heavily overnight and the workers hadn't yet cleared the snow from the streets. The nurse on duty noticed my stirrings and walked over. "You're awake! How do you feel?" she asked.

I croaked out a reply. "I don't feel anything."

She checked my vital signs. "Uh huh. So, can you tell me what your pain level is, from one to ten, ten being severe?" She squatted next to my bedside and I heard what sounded like water running from a tap. I licked my dry lips. She stood, holding what looked like a clear hot water bottle filled with gold liquid.

"One," I said.

"Good!" She drew my attention to a cord that was placed on the bed near my right hand. There was a single button on the knob end of the cord. "It's for the IV beside you. When you push the button, it's going to send morphine into your body. Don't worry, there's no chance of overdosing because it only sends out controlled amounts. But just use it when you need. Are you thirsty? I can get you some ice." She stepped out of the room in an efficient blur of pastel colours.

I'd had salpingectomy surgery using the laparotomy method: a large incision was made through my lower abdomen wall to remove my ruptured fallopian tube. The water tap sound I'd heard was the draining of my catheter bag. My brothers and friends braved the freezing cold January weather to visit us. The only person I hadn't told of my attempts to get pregnant was my mother. It had been an uneasy shift in our close relationship when I'd come out as a lesbian. I feared that throwing lesbian parenting into the mix might destroy whatever fragments of connection still existed between us.

I needed my mother. I felt so raw and very little. She was shocked when I called her from my room on the second day of my stay. "Mom. *Byouin-ni iru.* Pregnant *datta.*" I'm in the hospital. I was pregnant.

"Oh!" she exclaimed. "Boyfriend-*iru?*" Do you have a boyfriend? Hope lifted the tone of her voice.

"No," I said. And here I stopped. "I'm hurting" is what I wanted to say, but what I managed was, "It's bad." And I cried, gripping the phone, rocking myself.

"Don't cry," she said, her voice breaking. "It will be alright."

When I returned home, I couldn't stand straight and walked in shuffling steps as it felt like an anchor had been sewn into my insides. During one friend's visit, I asked her to wipe me after I'd urinated, hovering above the toilet bowl, as I couldn't bend over. We giggled as she took to the task with such solemnity, dabbing the pee from my vulva. My mother was coming over daily with home-cooked meals of Japanese food. *Goma-ae, nishime, shiozake:* sesame spinach salad, simmered chicken with root vegetables (carrots, burdock, *daikon*), grilled salted salmon. Each warm umami-flavoured morsel was like a comforter around my shoulders. She stayed just long enough to watch me eat a few bites. We were a family of few words, so the quiet between us wasn't unusual. But on the fourth day, she was in a mood to talk. She asked, "*Dou* pregnant *naru?*" How do you get pregnant? She was curious, but I detected something else in her question.

"Artificial insemination," I said.

Her brow furrowed. She didn't understand.

"A man donated his sperm and it gets put inside me. The baby and donor-father won't know each other," I explained.

"*Kawai-sou.*" Poor thing, she sighed.

I frowned. In the next instant, she opened her coat, lifted her red sweatshirt and pulled down the waistband of her polyester pants. "*Onnaji kizuato aru?*" I was thrown by her atypical intimacy.

She laughed and redressed herself. I had a rare glimpse of her faded scar, a remnant from the hysterectomy she'd had when she was in her thirties.

"Yes, I have the same scar, Mom," I said.

She nodded, satisfied. "Shall I give you a sponge bath?" she asked.

"No, I'm okay." She wanted to do more but I didn't want to overburden her.

"I'm going home then," she said. I opened the door for her and watched as she took each step of the wooden stairs carefully, holding onto the railing. The streets were slippery with brown slush and I worried that she might fall. She turned and waved goodbye before turning the corner.

I was on the phone with my mom the next morning. I had managed to step into the tub to have a hot shower and was seated in an armchair, my long wet hair rolled in a fluffy towel on top of my head. She was relaying her planned menu for the week. "*Nikujaga, kabocha no nimono, saba misoni.*" (Meat and potatoes, simmered Japanese pumpkin, mackerel in miso sauce.) I was touched by her attention. "And also," she added. "Your child won't be my grandchild." She emphasized "won't be." *De wa nai.*

I was stunned.

"Hello?" she said.

How long had she wanted to say this? "I know, Mom! Don't you think I know that? Why are you cooking for me?" I couldn't breathe. "Did you say this to your son when they had their kid?" I rose on shaky legs. "It's because I'm a lesbian, isn't it!" I slammed the phone onto its cradle. Then I wailed, clutching my injured belly as my body shook. And when the towel fell from my head onto the floor, I left it there. I threw out the Tupperware containers of leftovers she'd placed in our fridge.

Growing up in a tiny village in Kagoshima Prefecture, Japan, in the thirties, my mother was a feisty tomboy. She defended smaller children at school from the bullies, boys who quickly learnt that she wasn't afraid to fight. There was one stocky boy, Minoru, his name meaning "to bear fruit," that she challenged, standing in defence of a scared child. "*Mino-ran*," she'd tease him, changing the suffix to reflect the verb's negative. Infertile. Impotent. Doesn't bear fruit. She dared his balled-up fists and bullhead. Her parents were subsistence farmers and fisher folk, and when she was fourteen, without telling them, she quit school in order to move miles away and live in a dormitory with dozens of other poor girls who worked at a candy factory. She wasn't the eldest daughter in her family, for whom this act of sacrifice would've made sense, but she was the closest to her mother and knew her parents' financial struggles. Her teacher bicycled that evening to their dirt-floor home to beg her to stay because she showed such promise. But she refused. My mother loved every minute of school. She was the first to raise her hand in class and took her studies seriously. "I told my teacher no," my mom said. And I caught a glimpse of the girl who'd stood up to bullies.

She immigrated to Canada in the fifties as a twenty-one-year-old "picture bride," meaning that a relative organized the exchange of her photo with potential suitors both locally and away. My parents selected each other out of a pool of three prospective matches, and she travelled by ship to marry my father, a man she'd never met in a country she'd never been. They divorced twenty years later, as he turned out to be an abusive alcoholic like her father. As a family, we endured judgment from the Japanese-Canadian and larger community who deemed her a bad wife and mother. My father died at the age of fifty-eight in 1992, after his second divorce. I believe he loved his children. He taught us how to make origami animals and draw objects using a sharp lead pencil, but he terrorized us with his weekly rages. My mother was afraid of him until the day he died. Prior to his death, he managed to stammer an apology to me for his abusive behaviour toward her and for its impact on my brothers and me. I accepted his admission. He couldn't change or erase the past. For a long time, I saw him as my father through biology alone. Officially he died of heart disease, but I believe he died of a broken heart. I adored and hated him.

I felt like a loser, a failure at being a woman. Shame was a poison-tip arrow lodged in my throat and I found it difficult to swallow or speak. The sutures were removed a few weeks later by the operating surgeon, the yelling female voice from the hospital.

"Get back on the saddle and try again," she said.

I was grim in front of her chirpiness but I managed to widen my eyes and upturn the corners of my mouth into what I hoped was a reasonable smile. She had saved my life, after all. Prior to this, I had seen my family doctor who had read the operating notes. "You got to the hospital just in time. Another twenty minutes and we wouldn't be sitting here," she said. "How's your sleep? Your eating patterns?" She took in my slumped shoulders and dishevelled appearance. I was still sore and my hormones were off balance, which led to dizzy spells, anxiety and insomnia. She prescribed a low dosage of Ativan that offered some relief from my symptoms.

I isolated myself and leaned too much on my partner, who was also grieving. I was demanding, exhausting. My community at that time was other lesbian and heterosexual couples who were successfully growing their families. My monthly budget expanded to include baby shower gifts, although I attended none of these gatherings. I assume that I was deemed anti-social at best, and that I hated children at worst. I was mostly in the closet, as it were, about my infertility story. I didn't want to be pitied or make others feel uncomfortable by my presence, especially at a time of joyous celebration.

It's not true that women who've had abortions don't think about and sometimes agonize over their decision. Part of my grief recovery meant ruminating over the pregnancy I'd terminated in the eighties. Why didn't I have the baby? Why was I so arrogant to think I could have a baby any time I wanted to? Who would my child have been? Who would I have been? I had a choice then of how to deal with an unplanned pregnancy and, as with every choice, it carried a set of consequences. I came to the conclusion that even if I were able to return to the past, with the full knowledge of my life now, I'd make the same decision. I am not a mother. I am infertile, impotent, a barren fruit. *Mino-ran.* My mother's story comes back to haunt me.

I tried one more time to get pregnant in the summer of 2000. I had survived the acute stages of my grief. What had eased my distress were the writings of women who had also dealt with infertility and pregnancy loss. From an early age, I had sought solace in books and it was there again I found comfort. This, and the quiet conversations I was having with others in a similar state, were integral to my healing. I wasn't alone, and I wasn't a freak. Back at the clinic, I stared at the ceiling as Donna, the lab technician, moved the condom-wrapped ultrasound probe into my vagina. The only sounds came from the crinkling of the crepe paper as I shifted my position on the examining table. I turned my head and saw a mini universe on the portable TV-sized screen. Fertility circles in the celestial heavens, curving canals and pulsing shapes surrounded by pricks of light. She magnified the image of the right side of my uterus. The ovary connected to my remaining fallopian tube contained several follicles. "We're in luck," she said. She removed the probe and replaced it in its holster on one side of the machine. "Don't give up hope. We had a woman with five ectopic pregnancies, but she's now in the third trimester of a pregnancy. And remember, there's always in vitro fertilization." It was my last unsuccessful attempt. As a couple we were too financially and emotionally exhausted to contemplate any other paths to parenthood. I was ready and wanting to move on, too.

In February 2001, I became an aunt again. Since my mom's stinging declaration the previous year, I rarely initiated contact with her and any conversations we had were brief and formal. My brother invited my partner and me to meet their second child at her place. "We're thinking of the name Akemi for her middle name. What do you think?" he asked me.

My mom and I gasped and looked at each other. "That's my name!" I said.

"Oh, yeah." My brother blushed. When my mother was born, the midwife who delivered her told my grandmother to call her Akemi, but she had already chosen a name. My mom later acknowledged the midwife's role by passing on the name to me. There's a photo from that visit and in it I look startlingly young and happy, staring at my newborn niece who's in my arms.

I was raised with my parents' rural Japanese folk traditions that valued connection, continuity and community. As a teenager, I remember my brothers and me finding what looked like three individually wrapped dried worms as we rummaged through a storage bin, looking for some item or another. We shrieked at our find and dared one another to touch them. These shrivelled scraps of skin were each of her three children's *o-heso-no-o*, literally, "the tail of" (*no-o*) the "belly button" (*o-heso*), that bit of umbilical cord that falls from a baby's belly a week after its birth. Rooted in Japan's sentimental view of the bond between a mother and her child, even into adulthood, it is honoured and saved for posterity. When we approached Mom with what we found, she demystified the preserved fragments with an explanation and restored them to their delicate onion skin paper casings. I never saw them again.

In my efforts to erase any evidence of my inadequacy, I swabbed my crimson abdominal scar with vitamin E cream. It was hidden by dark pubic hairs and puckered slightly at each end; it itched when I ovulated. A psychic called it my "mark," an emblem of my courage and resolve.

I wanted to make peace with my mom. It was a lot of work to pretend that I didn't miss her. I was still upset, but I knew that while she wasn't perfect, she wasn't a mean person. She knew what it meant to not be reliant on a man. That I was a lesbian wasn't something she'd hoped for, but she put aside her discomfort because I was her daughter. And it was impossible to know whether she really would've rejected my child as she'd threatened to. She turned sixty-five in June 2002, and with her first government pension cheque, she bought me a top-of-the-line vacuum cleaner. "I could never afford to buy you anything," she said. My mom cleaned houses for a living and took great pride in a job well done. The gift was both practical and symbolic. It was her apology. For her birthday we barbecued a large salmon at our place and sang a rousing "Happy Birthday" to her as I brought out the ice-cream cake that she'd requested, for her grandchildren's enjoyment. I had seen her only once, at Christmas break, since my niece's birth, and seated beside me now, she appeared different somehow, shrunken.

In July 2003, my mom was diagnosed with terminal pancreatic cancer and passed away in palliative care nine months later. It was brutally quick. I am not proud of the fact that at times I was impatient with her and scolded her as if she were an unruly child. No matter how much I tried to convince myself that she hadn't hurt me, I struggled with my residual resentment and hated myself for it. Before the disease had debilitated her, leaving her frail and fragile, I had taken her grocery shopping where she ran into a friend.

"*Watashi-no musumedesu,*" she said. Her small hand squeezed my arm. Her eyes were bright and clear as she beamed.

Her friend exclaimed with delight. "Your daughter!" I was surprised by my mother's obvious pride. I stayed with her in the hospital in the final weeks of her life and apologized to her for being such a bad daughter, for my lapses in kindness.

"We've said all we need to say to each other," she said. We can't change or erase the past. Her suffering ended on the first warm spring day in 2004. My partner and I separated two years later.

I wipe tears from my face. The water of the bay sparkles as cut diamonds in the sun. I watch a Frisbee fly overhead, landing on someone's towel. The goose down has disappeared, the sand kicked up by a passing boy. I bend the charred piece of goatskin into a crescent shape. To recognize my identity as a post-menopausal woman, and in honour of my mom's thirteenth Buddhist memorial anniversary (or twelve full years from death), I burned the goatskin, my imagined o-heso-no-o, *to symbolize releasing the past to make way for the present. From being mothered to being a motherless child to being a woman who is not a mother. I let go.*

ATTACHMENT ROULETTE

Marusya Bociurkiw

The first time I met her, she slid her arms around me.

"Awww," I said.

Bree, the social worker: "Isn't that sweet."

I'd been at it for three years. Adoption. Orientation, paperwork, a mandatory seminar on parenting — scary stories on blurry VHS videos; Cassie, the sketchy model foster mom ("I take their phones away if they're even one minute late for breakfast; it's for their own good"); a PowerPoint about attachment theory. We prospective parents gazed, wide-eyed, at a bright circle of arrows illustrating how the child would push us away and then come back, only to push us away again, the arrows circulating, stopping, starting. Attachment roulette, I called it.

The other parental candidates: nervous smiles, best behaviour. I wondered at motivation: the white Christian couple that prayed every night for The Lord to send their adoptive child to them, wannabe Dad wearing a T-shirt with "Jesus Saves" in huge Coca-Cola script. The older South Asian couple I met in the cafeteria lineup during break. "He needs something to occupy him since retirement," said the wife, as she slammed a Morning Glory muffin onto her tray.

There was only one other single woman at the parenting seminar besides me. I sidled up to her in the cafeteria. Felicity. A criminal lawyer. She was gaming for a baby. The highest prize. I adored Felicity's earnestness, her solemn belief in herself, even her occasional flashes of righteous anger. Chewing on my chicken Caesar wrap, I hung on to her every word. "You really have to network with the social workers, so they think of you when a kid comes up

… It's basically a super-long pregnancy … I told my family, if you don't accept this child then you sure as hell won't be seeing me!"

I had just bought my first house, and I had moved in that week. I made nice with no social worker, uttered no prayer. I did not examine my own motivation, and no one asked me to.

The house had an extra room, for the child. That first month, a cardinal tapped incessantly at the window, flashing red like a tidy splatter of blood.

In my spare time, I scoured websites with photographs of sweetly smiling children. Like a dating site, but with kids: illicit-feeling, with overtones of trafficking. I went to an adoption fair in a hotel ballroom. In the company of hundreds of childless couples, I leafed through catalogues of available kids. The dry, hungry sound of all those hands flipping through pages. The whispered comments: "She's so cute." "He's adorable." I visited the adjoining ballroom that had booths from various regions, social workers standing at each one. In a catalogue I'd found a picture and description of a child that I liked. The child's name was Sofia. Sofia held a hand puppet in her photo. It made you remember the photo. Sofia had strategy.

I followed the trail to a booth with the name Catholic Children's Aid. Dissociated, drunk with desire, I chatted with a social worker named Maria. She wore a brooch of praying hands on her grey serge lapel. I filled out forms and spoke with Maria on the phone several times after the fair. I did not mention that I am a lesbian.

I got bumped for a straight couple with two children. I did some research: Catholic Children's Aid does not discriminate against homosexuals. It simply follows church law.

A social worker was appointed to me. Selena. Dull-eyed and placid, Selena showed up for regular interviews at my house. That was part of the standard agency process. Selena hunched limply over a yellow legal pad: "What was your relationship like with your mother?" "Paint a picture for me." I always had a plate of fresh baked muffins or cookies on the table. Selena never touched my baking. Six months later, Selena had still not written her report.

I demanded a new social worker.

Bree showed up at my door on a fresh spring morning: tired eyes, sincere smile, long, shiny black hair. Bree ate my muffins ravenously.

Bree was pragmatic and thought outside the box. Despite the agency's taboo on cross-racial adoption, and despite my desire for a younger child, Bree found me a Malaysian teenager. At our second meeting, she handed me a document with both hands, like a gift. Eighteen pages long, it summed up the girl's entire history, including years of abuse suffered at the hands of her family. It deployed careful, archaic and often sentimental prose. *She is a pleasant young lady. She likes to cook. She is a very likeable, sweet girl.* There were one or two mentions of her refusing to attend school and of running away from foster homes. When I inquired, Bree said, "Oh, don't worry. The current foster mom is a bit neglectful. We really feel that with you she will be fine."

By then, I had been trying to adopt for four years ("... basically a super long pregnancy ..."). Did I want to meet the girl? Bree asked. I said yes.

Two days after Christmas, Bree dropped Cindi off for our first one-on-one visit. Four-foot-nothing, cloud of black hair, a dimpled smile. I made her a hot turkey sandwich. "Ooooh, this is sooo good," she said. We talked about school, her life, my work. She was into cooking, makeup and astrology. She told me about a friend of hers who had made a homophobic comment and how, in response, she brought him to the Pride Parade. I beamed. I gave her a gift, a woollen infinity scarf. Instead of putting it around her neck, she wrapped it like a kind of turban on her head. It was a beautiful, original thing to do with that scarf.

Our visits continued into the new year and got longer, like the days themselves. I'd meet her for Chinese food downtown, or take her out for hot chocolate after a meeting with Bree. At one of those agency meetings, I met the foster mom, Sadie. Sadie was a retired secretary, working class, statuesque, sarcastic. We took the elevator down to the ground floor together. She looked me over and said in a husky smoker's voice, "She's been cryin' herself to sleep all week." Cindi had been with her for three years.

As we said goodbye on the street she touched my arm and said, doubtfully, "I wish ya luck."

One day, after some coaching by Bree, I asked Cindi if she'd like to be part of a "forever family." By then it was summer. We were sitting in a park eating organic ice cream. "Huh?" she asked.

"I mean, adoption," I said. "You and me. We'd be a family."

"Oh," she said. She licked her ice cream nervously and looked off into the distance, squinting. "Sure, I'd like that."

Bree started the paperwork. I left the country on a research trip. While I was away, Bree emailed to tell me the girl had changed her mind. Stranded in a small city in Ukraine, I shed some tears and threw myself back into my work.

Four months later, Bree called again, out of the blue. Would I consider fostering Cindi? I didn't even think about it. I said yes.

Bree started new paperwork. I had lunch with Cindi. She apologized: "I wasn't ready." I gave her the embroidered blouse I'd bought for her on my trip. "Ooooh, that's so cute," she said.

Cindi came over for a series of overnight stays. The first time, she brought a shopping bag full of books. She went to her room and spent an hour carefully placing the books into a bookshelf. That night, we made veggie pizza together and she told me the story of her life so far — the one I had read about in the documents, but without the sentimentality. Then we watched an Audrey Hepburn movie together. I didn't know if she'd like it. I watched her as she laughed and laughed.

The next morning, Cindi came down in her pyjamas and asked if she could please make breakfast. She cooked me blueberry pancakes with maple syrup, while playing YouTube videos of her favourite hip hop music. She asked me what kind of music I like, and then found it on YouTube: Miles Davis, *Kind of Blue*. Sadie came to pick her up and waited in the car. As usual, Cindi hugged me goodbye. This time she looked at me and said, "Thank you. I had a very nice time."

We went to the art gallery, discussed Jean-Michel Basquiat. We marched together on International Women's Day. I bought her a T-shirt that said, "Women United Will Never Be Defeated."

Cindi moved in on Valentine's Day. I made hot turkey sandwiches again and, for fun, heart-shaped sugar cookies. Bree joined us for lunch. "Isn't this delicious?" Bree said. Cindi was silent. "Wasn't it nice of your new foster mom to make these cookies?" The girl sighed irritably, looked away.

She went to unpack her suitcases. She stayed there all afternoon, didn't come down for dinner. She went to bed early.

The next day, Cindi refused to go to school, locking herself in her room, mummified in sheets in a room fetid with perfume and sweat. On Bree's advice, I left bowls of food outside the door and texted her, slipping x's and o's into wary messages.

She stopped eating breakfast. She refused the packed lunches I made. At night she tiptoed downstairs to make herself some rice. She said rice was comforting, reminded her of Malaysia. I did research: books on normal teens, troubled teens, adopted and fostered teens. I scoured the Internet for information on Malaysian food and culture. I started to make *nasi goreng* every week.

Some days I hid from her, usually after she skipped school. Her girlish voice singing along to funk music in her room all afternoon reminded me of my own maternal shortcomings. My parents got me to school: I should be able to achieve at least as much. I went to my room, put headphones on, worked on my laptop. When I did this, she would knock on my door to tell me something I already knew, like her working hours the next day.

All this intimacy and banal caregiving, the buying of juice boxes and mini-yogurts, the uncounted hours sitting around and talking about nothing. This, as I understood it, was family life: terrifying, for different reasons, to both of us.

But the books said: consequences. So, I changed the Internet password a half-dozen times, cycling through the names of fruits she loved — strawberry, pineapple, dragon fruit — so she couldn't go online. The first time I did this she screamed at me, voice wild and frightened. The next day she went to school.

I was on a new project that required me to work late, but when I came home, there she was, still up, in the wicker chair that she said reminded her of her childhood. Her head was always bowed over her phone, its secret messages of desire and temporary belonging illuminating her small, heart-shaped face. I'd heat up some *nasi goreng*, ask her if she wanted any. "No, I'm good," not looking at me.

"How was school?"

"Fine."

I kept talking, in a calm, grey voice, not knowing if she was listening. I talked about what happened in my life that morning or the day before. I tried to pass on words, talismans I hoped might protect her in her journey. *Catharsis. Respect.* I told her why we use plates, or why it's important to forgive.

If I sat as far away from her as possible, avoiding eye contact, she'd talk to me. Memories from Malaysia, where she lived until the age of six. A beautiful waterfall her grandmother used to take her to. The congee her aunt cooked, you couldn't get congee anywhere like that in Toronto.

After one of those random evenings of intimacy, she came downstairs wearing sunglasses and a hoodie, face swollen with belligerent anger, mouth tight as a drawstring. She ate some pineapple I had left out for her over the sink. She left the house without saying goodbye, door slamming behind her.

We settled into a kind of routine. She would ignore me for days, and then grant me a late-night conversation. The more frank or intimate the exchange, the harder she'd lash back the next day. She told the social workers I wasn't feeding her. She told me that she'd never enjoyed my meals.

One month after she moved in, Bree called. "There's something I need to tell you," she said. "Please don't take it personally."

Cindi had told Bree that she fantasized stabbing me with a knife or pushing me down the stairs.

I put my knives in a locked drawer. I started locking my bedroom at night. I never spoke to Cindi about this. I wasn't afraid of physical harm. Rather, I was afraid of the crumbling of my self-esteem.

She got a job at a fast food court. She would rush out of the house in her uniform, shouting her schedule at me as she left.

I had been single for five years. That spring I met someone. A woman in the same field of work as me, who had a teenaged daughter. We met for coffee. As I told her about my failed attempts at parenting, I could feel salt water welling in my eyes. Even so, she invited me out for dinner. I asked Cindi if she would help me prepare for my date. "I don't think so." I offered her fifteen dollars for a pedicure.

It was one of the first warm days of spring: lime green leaves, a soft wind. Sparrows, blue jays. The flash of a cardinal. We sat outside on the deck as she painted my toenails blue. More stories about Malaysia: her uncle who taught underwater diving, her cousin who was a dress designer. She said she was thinking about moving back to Kuala Lumpur and working for her cousin; she was sure the cousin would offer her a job. It was her plan to be living on her own in two years; she was saving up money, she'd support herself and her mom, too. It was her dream.

Two weeks after that date, and three months after moving in, Cindi did not come home after school. I left a message for Bree. I waited and waited, texting the girl repeatedly. *Where are you. Are you okay? Did something happen? Please just let me know that you're okay. Xo.*

She texted me at midnight. *I m @ Sadie's, I never wanted 2 live w u. Pls lv me alone.*

I went into her room, threw open the closet door. I don't know why I hadn't thought to do it earlier. It was empty of clothes. The makeup and nail polish that had cluttered her desk had vanished. There was a faint, fruity smell of perfume.

On the bed, laid out like a message: an infinity scarf, an embroidered blouse, a feminist T-shirt.

Bree called first thing in the morning. I told her Cindi should stay with Sadie. That she should never have been made to leave Sadie.

Bree came over for a final session of tea and cookies. "I'm so sorry it didn't work out. Don't take it personally."

I keep seeing that roulette wheel. The click and clatter of it. Its rewards, its dangers. Its infinite movement. The wheel going in one direction, the spinning ball in another. The rush of dopamine when you get it right, the crashing adrenaline afterwards.

What she taught me. What I taught her.

The hope that the gains will overcome the losses eventually.

Double Rainbow Baby

Amanda Roth

I. The Road to Queer Baby-Making

My wife, Rachel, and I met in 2005 while preparing for a party. I was running cheap, bright blue vodka through a Brita filter when Rachel — the roommate of a friend's long-distance significant other — arrived. A flirtation developed quickly and after consuming a lot of that vodka, I danced around a makeshift maypole and told Rachel all about my ovulation cycle — or so she tells me.

Fast-forward six years and my ovulation cycle was on our minds again — this time to make a baby. Neither of us had expected anything to come out of that early flirtation-turned-casual-sex relationship, so it didn't much matter that we were at first on very different pages when it came to planning for a family. I was sure I wanted to be a parent, but sometime *well* into the future, while Rachel was not so interested. But casual sex became a long-term relationship, and by 2011 we were in a completely different life- and relationship-stage. True to many lesbian stereotypes, we'd been living together since early in the relationship and had recently moved to a house, providing more space for our growing gaggle of (often disabled) pets. I had completed my PhD and was looking for a job as a philosopher in the depths of the recession and Rachel had successfully changed careers to enter the IT world. We'd also, despite various misgivings about marriage as an institution, tied the knot legally in Massachusetts in 2010.

By this point, Rachel especially felt her motherhood clock ticking away at thirty-four. I was more hesitant, being six years younger and hoping to establish my career before having children, but my career prospects seemed to sink each year. And so, in contrast to my usual overly cautious self, I said yes to Rachel and we took the leap. As I was the younger of us, had fewer health problems and was unable (at the time) to provide a decent income, I was an obvious choice for who would gestate.

So, we did what you do when you are queer cis women looking to have a baby: scoured message boards about trying to conceive, studied insemination success rates, tracked my basal body temperature and cervical mucus, and began imagining the new person we might create. We also thought long and hard about sperm: known donor or bank? Anonymous or open identity? How to choose amongst so many possible donors? Through all of this planning and decision-making, our queerness was at the forefront of our minds. It was as if we had entered the next stage of life for LBQ women couples: love, marriage (in six states at the time, at least) and then the turkey baster.

Though in fact, Rachel and I were not in agreement about the turkey baster (okay, "needleless syringe"). I leaned toward the old-fashioned DIY method, while Rachel was attracted to intra-uterine insemination (IUI) performed by a doctor, given its slight advantage in likelihood of conception. To help us decide, we scheduled an appointment with a reproductive endocrinologist (RE) for a check-up of sorts; we planned to request some basic blood testing to screen for fertility red flags and to get an expert view on IUI versus DIY insemination.

Our appointment took place about a month before we planned to begin trying to conceive. It started out on a positive note. Much to our relief we didn't face any hostility or discomfort on account of our sexuality; the clinic seemed to welcome us as a same-sex couple (this was Ann Arbor, Michigan, after all). But other aspects of the visit left much to be desired: while we were undecided about whether to pursue a medicalized or DIY approach to reproduction, the specialists clearly saw the former as a foregone conclusion. The RE brushed off questions about how to time home insemination, talking to us only about IUI. He also insisted that I undergo further testing of my uterus — a hysterosalpingogram (HSG) — given fibroids in my medical history, though I questioned the necessity of such testing. I left the appointment disappointed and feeling pressured to take up medical intervention that was unwanted and seemed unnecessary. Fibroids were very common, my charts were perfect and my ovulation prediction kit (OPK) turned positive on cue. I ranted: "I have never even had sperm in my vagina! So, why am I being treated like a fertility patient when there is no evidence of a fertility problem?" Rachel saw my point, but reasoned that the testing was just a hoop we might as well jump through to get access to IUI, if we decided we wanted it.

A few weeks later, our unease with the clinic entered full panic territory. A nurse called and reported that a Day 21 progesterone test showed low progesterone levels, indicating no or low quality ovulation. They were prescribing Clomid, an ovulation-stimulating drug. She said little else about how the drug worked or its risks or benefits; instead, before hanging up, she once again reminded me that I hadn't scheduled the HSG, and reiterated that the RE refused to perform an IUI until the test was completed. I had expected that the prescription of fertility drugs would at least involve a conversation about weighing options and considering risks and benefits. Not to mention, we had never actually said we wanted an IUI! But in fact, neither the IUI, nor the HSG, nor Clomid were presented as options; the implication seemed to be that this path, set by the RE without any input from us, was *the* way to conceive.

After this phone call we were of two minds. The low progesterone result sent us into a spiral of doubt about my fertility and whether attempting DIY would be a waste of time and money. Yet simultaneously, the bioethicist in me (bioethics being one of my research and teaching areas) was outraged at the clinic's ignoring our own stated aims, pressuring us into interventions and prescribing medication without discussing serious risks, especially the risk of a multiple pregnancy. Again, I wondered, *Would a straight woman ever be prescribed Clomid on the basis of one blood test, having never actually attempted to conceive?*

This time Rachel was onboard with me — we were not willing to increase our chance of a multiple pregnancy on the first attempt at conceiving. We knew it was common for LBQ women who pursued medicalized reproduction to have multiples; we wondered if this might often be the result of pressure to take up medical interventions, as we'd experienced. Were LBQ women in general, in being placed in a fertility patient paradigm, being over-treated? In any case, we did not want that for ourselves, and so we agreed: no fertility meds until trying for at least a month or two without them.

And so, we forged ahead: when the OPK strip turned purple, we inseminated once that evening and once the next morning. We were scared, hopeful and exhilarated all at once. A few days later, as I walked the dog down the street, I felt an odd cramping in my lower left pelvis. The blogs I was scouring during the two-week wait talked about implantation cramping, but it seemed too early for that. *Yet surely it must mean something*, I thought. At eight days post-ovulation, I broke the first rule of the two-week wait — don't test too early — and peed on a stick. Unsurprisingly it showed nothing. Early the next morning, I took another test. Though it was still far too early to expect a positive result, this time I got one. It was extremely pale, but it was there. I ran to deliver the news to a still sleeping Rachel. We had done it! I was pregnant! And on the first try!

We were elated, but I was also nervous. I immediately worried — what the universe had given us, the universe could also take away. What if I had a miscarriage? I knew they were common in the first trimester, especially the first few weeks, so I continued to take pregnancy tests every day for a while to ensure that the line still appeared. The nausea in week six was unpleasant but also a relief: it was a comforting indication of high HCG levels, and an indication of a progressing pregnancy.

We also got our first look inside the womb later that week, and what a surprise we found: *two* embryonic sacs! One sac housed a typically developing embryo whose heart was fluttering away.

The other appeared to be empty, with no fetal pole or heartbeat detectable. "Probably vanishing twin syndrome," we were told. "It's not uncommon. Many people don't even realize it's happened unless they have an early ultrasound. You can expect the second sac will likely disappear within a few weeks."

This was an odd experience. I had been fearing pregnancy loss so strongly, and now we were technically experiencing a pregnancy loss — the failure of one conceptus to develop into an embryo. Yet it didn't feel like a loss; it felt like something that never began in the first place. We happily wished the empty sac away, glad to know there was one — and only one — baby on the way.

But the surprises were far from over. At eight weeks we had another ultrasound to confirm that the second sac had disappeared. Imagine our shock when, as the image appeared on the screen, the ultrasound tech announced, "There they both are." *Both?!*, Rachel and I simultaneously thought, too shocked to speak. Indeed, this time there were two sacs, but also two embryos and two fluttering hearts. Twins!

After the shock wore off and we informed our families about this surprising turn of events, I became all the more indignant about our experience at the RE clinic. Here I was, pregnant on the first un-medicated attempt with *two* babies! And while it couldn't be 100 percent confirmed, it was very likely that these were fraternal twins, meaning I had released two eggs. And yet, had I taken the advice of the RE, I would have used Clomid that month. What would the result have been then? Might I have ended up pregnant with quintuplets?!

This experience has been fodder for some of my own scholarly work within bioethics, and as such, I have heard many other stories along the same lines. More and more, LBQ women's reproduction has become medicalized, and new reproductive technological options are likely to continue this trend. In fact, whenever the topic came up for Rachel and me in everyday life, the assumption seemed to be that medicalization was the norm for LBQ women looking to have children. Often (especially straight, cis) folks even seemed more comfortable with the idea of queer reproduction as a medical event than in DIY form. It was as if the image of the doctor stood in for the assumed naturalness of heterosexual sex in traditional baby-making. Given this, it was fun at times to see the looks on people's faces when we told them about having sperm delivered to our home and doing the rest ourselves. Although we hadn't set out to make a political point in choosing a DIY approach, we found that conceiving in this way only seemed to heighten the queerness of what we were doing.

II. THE STORM

But what about the rest of the tale? What of those babies we were expecting? How did things end? Ah, but the story has only just begun.

After discovering twins, we went about adjusting our plans and expectations with two babies in mind. My fears of losing the pregnancy ratcheted up since multiple pregnancies carry increased risk. Yet at the same time that I felt unsure the pregnancy would be successful, the thought and hope that it would be — and that two babies would result — drove us into early preparation mode, even with weeks left to reach the second-trimester hurdle. Meanwhile my morning sickness increased, leading me to give up a decade of vegetarianism in a shameful moment with a McDonald's hamburger. I also puzzled over how to hide a twin pregnancy during the academic job interviews I had coming up. (Answer: be fat already.) And more generally, we tried to take in everything we could about pregnancy, birth and parenting of multiples. Eventually, after what seemed an eternity, the second-trimester was upon us — a great relief. We had made it through the danger period. This was really happening: two babies!

And then, at fourteen weeks, another surprise — a bad one. At a routine ultrasound, Baby A was doing fine, but our provider stopped in her tracks when she moved the wand to the other side of my abdomen toward Baby B. We could tell immediately that this was not good. Baby B had no heartbeat, a higher-level ultrasound confirmed an hour later. We were experiencing vanishing twin syndrome after all. But everything was different now: despite our having done all we could to avoid a multiple pregnancy and having hoped for the supposedly empty sac to disappear, we had for weeks been expecting, planning for and loving two babies. Now we had lost one of them, along with a particular future as the parents of multiples that had begun to take shape.

Despite the pain of this loss, it seemed best to shift our attention to Baby A. We were still going to be parents after all. An ultrasound at sixteen weeks to check out Baby A's development raised no red flags. The ultrasound technician was also able to confirm the baby's "hamburger," allowing us to settle on a name we had always loved: Alice. Our future child was coming more and more into view. Meanwhile, the holidays came and went. Family gifts centered on the coming baby and out of town friends threw us a mini baby shower. This was all bittersweet given the baby we had just lost. We tried to keep up our spirits, yet I couldn't shake the feeling that tragedy might strike at any moment. By every medical indication all was fine; if anything, there was less risk overall of a bad outcome in a singleton pregnancy. Yet, no matter how many reassurances we received — including a perfect anatomy scan — I was always waiting for the other shoe to drop.

And at eighteen and a half weeks it did. On the morning of January 5, I felt an odd back pain. Hours later the pain was still there and coming rhythmically. My obstetrician-gynaecologist's office was not overly concerned, but suggested I go to the Labour and Delivery unit just in case. By the time we arrived, the pain had substantially intensified and I began vomiting, leading Rachel and me to panic. The medical professionals there were puzzled as to what was happening. The ultrasound showed our baby still squirming, looking perfectly healthy. Perhaps a gastrointestinal virus or a kidney stone, they suggested hopefully. Eventually, though, it became clear that I was in labour when my water broke and my cervix was discovered to be significantly dilated. We knew there were no options at that gestation — the baby could not survive. After labouring all day, I delivered her around 10:30 p.m. that evening. She was ten inches long and weighed about half a pound. Though she was alive and kicking just hours earlier, by the time she exited my body she had no heartbeat. We held her and examined her body. And then the next morning, we walked out of the hospital — me no longer pregnant, but also with no baby.

This loss was a pain like none we had ever experienced before or since. I could think of nothing else for months. We struggled to make sense of what it meant: Was it a miscarriage? A stillbirth? Did we lose a fetus? Or a baby? Should we name her? How do we tell others what happened? Nothing was clear. Having a pregnancy loss of any kind is lonely, but a loss of this kind seemed almost unheard of. Literally no one we knew had a story like ours — not only of preterm labour at eighteen and a half weeks, but also a loss of two babies in one pregnancy just a month apart. I spent days crying on the couch and we struggled to try to regain a sense of normal life.

When good queer friends of ours announced their own pregnancy a few months later, I could (shamefully, in retrospect) find nothing but jealousy in myself. Instead of feeling part of a community of queer parents-to-be, we felt like outsiders. Suddenly we no longer viewed everything pregnancy- and parenting-related through the lens of our sexual identity; a new identity seemed more relevant, an identity as people who'd experienced a devastating loss that shook our confidence in our ability to become parents at all. We eventually found a very helpful pregnancy loss support group. It was a relief to simply be around other people like us, to be open and honest about what we were going through, and to feel like others "got it."

Attending the support group was a very odd experience. Rachel and I were anything but "group" kind of people, and it had been a long time since I had felt that any group of straight couples and women could better "get" me than close queer friends. I did not make the connection at the time, but in retrospect our relationship to queerness at this point in our lives had become much more complex. These months were the least gay I had felt since college, when I first came out. It was as if the queerness of our identities receded to the background of our lives. What had previously made us the odd ones out — being two women in love, getting married, trying to get me pregnant, expecting a child — was now so much less relevant. We were now the odd ones out even within the queer community it seemed, as almost-sort-of-but-not-really mothers. I had given birth, we had held a baby, we had footprints, we had named her, but still we were childless.

III. SEEKING A DOUBLE RAINBOW

Five months after delivering Alice, we were both finally ready to try again. It was surreal to be back where we were almost one year before. And as conceiving became the primary focus of our lives again and we were back to (re)choosing a donor and undertaking a DIY insemination, our relationship with queerness shifted once more. This time we felt our queerness in both senses: we were looking for a rainbow baby in the sense of creating a child as a same-sex couple, but also a rainbow in the post-loss sense — a rainbow after the storm of pregnancy loss.

I turned up pregnant after the second month of trying. This began the longest nine months of our lives, which we lived in a constant sense of potential impending doom. We counted down each day, celebrated each pregnancy milestone, got lots of therapy, cried endless tears of anxiety and worry, and spent a lot of time in the Labour and Delivery unit for false alarms. By the end of the second-trimester, the alarms were no longer false. My cervix began funnelling and shortening, contractions set in and I started dilating around twenty-nine weeks. After a night hospitalized while my uterus calmed down, I was told to take it easy and stop commuting the hour to my teaching position in rural Ohio. There was no predicting what would happen, the doctors told us. The baby could come any day, or she might stick around to term. So many old fears returned, but we took comfort in knowing we were well into the territory of viability, should the baby indeed arrive early.

Each night we poked Ada through my belly and watched her vigorous movements, all while begging her to stay in. We set milestones for her: thirty-two weeks was a good first goal. At thirty-four they would no longer try to stop the labour. At thirty-six there would probably be no need to stay in the neonatal intensive care unit. And thirty-seven — term — was all we even bothered to hope for. Imagine our surprise when we hit thirty-seven weeks, and still Ada remained inside, though my cervix was unmeasurable length-wise and a few inches dilated. "You can come now!" we began telling Ada.

But she didn't come. A new fear gripped us: there were ways to lose a baby other than preterm labour. Wouldn't it be the ultimate irony to have gotten past all of the windows of worry about prematurity and then to lose the baby at full term *inside* my body?

Finally, at thirty-nine weeks and four days, and after a total of over fifty-eight weeks of pregnancy including the first ill-fated pregnancy, Ada arrived in the world perfectly healthy, crying and *alive*. In the delivery room, Rachel, my mother and I all burst into tears of simultaneous relief, happiness and grief as Ada was placed on my chest. That first moment laying eyes on her — probably the best moment of my life — will forever be entangled emotionally with the worst — the moment in the same hospital, just over a year earlier, when Alice lifelessly exited my body. Appropriately, then, we gave Ada the middle name Alice, an ode to the baby who had come and gone before her.

It wasn't long after Ada's birth that we adjusted back to normal life — or at least a new normal, as we learned how to be parents. While we had all the usual new parent fears, we were no longer bracing ourselves for the worst. Breastfeeding woes, colic, finances and my lack of career prospects took up that space in our worrying. And, of course, there were special challenges in being queer parents. Filling out Ada's birth certificate in the hospital was the first of many (expected, but painful nonetheless) slaps in the face to Rachel, whom the state of Michigan refused to recognize as a parent. And as many same-sex couples find, making room for two people to play the role of mother — with all its cultural baggage — was a challenge, made all the worse as breastfeeding combined with my lack of employment and Rachel's lack of (paid) parental leave. But that we were able to even experience these sorts of problems was a testament to how much had changed with Ada's birth. No longer were we in a constant state of fear. We finally were parents.

IV. Living on the Other Side of the Rainbow

Looking back on our story, there's something intriguing about how the various phases of our becoming queer parents fit together. Much about our lives now is influenced by our queerness, from my teaching and research as a professor (philosophy and women's and gender studies), to legal issues we have faced as a family, to our parenting style with our five-year-old, to our seeking out community with other LGBTQ people. Queerness is often front and centre. And it was front and centre, as well, in the beginning of our story, in terms of our path to getting pregnant and our eventual embrace of the DIY route to conceiving.

And yet, queerness was also there in the middle part of our story, in a different sense. Our sense of outsiderness, of worrying about whether we were making others uncomfortable in pregnancy and parenting spaces, and of needing to be around others who "got it," was much less about our sexuality and much more about the experience of pregnancy loss during those months.

When I first began to reflect on our story of LGBTQ parenting, it was hard to see how the different parts of our story cohered. What did our pregnancy loss, after all, have to do with queerness? Sometimes in shaping our narrative, it's felt as if we have to choose: Either our story is one of parenting after loss or of LGBTQ parenting, so how can it be both? But I see now that both parts of our story can be connected by the symbol of the rainbow. For LGBTQ people, the rainbow represents our difference, our struggle and our strength as a community. For those having lost a pregnancy, the rainbow is a symbol of the possibility of future goodness. The beauty of a rainbow is possible only because of the storm that comes before, and difference, struggle and strength live in experiencing pregnancy loss as well. The different pieces of our history then actually cohere more than diverge. And that is the story of how we came to have our daughter Ada — our double rainbow baby.

How I (Finally) Became a Genderqueer Parent

Jo Jefferson

This is a story about big questions and awkward answers, about tricky conversations, shifting roles, a lot of sperm, and love. Mostly it's about love.

When Rachel and I had our earliest conversations about the possibility of her having a baby, I was fifty-two years old and Mom to two adult kids. She was pretty determined to have a baby, something she'd been planning to do since she was about sixteen, and now that her Bubby was in her nineties, she was feeling like the process of planning a baby should get started. The question she needed me to answer was, if she had a baby, what role would I play?

At first the idea of "being a parent again" seemed impossible. I was too old, I'd thought, for the energy demands, the sleeplessness, the years of diapers and schools and new shoes and college savings funds. I'd done all that and wasn't sure I wanted to do it again.

We went on a long walk after dark through our neighbourhood — passing the front gardens and porches of other houses, the lighted living rooms and kitchens, watching the shadows of strangers passing from room to room — and we talked about what might feel okay. I told her that because I loved her so much I wanted to support this desire she had to get pregnant. She was worried that I was just starting to really enjoy my independence from my kids now that they were adults supporting themselves. She thought that maybe I wouldn't want to be so tied down, that I would want to have lots of time to write all the books I'd described to her from my imagination. I told her I thought I could be her partner while she had a baby, but I was not sure I could be a parent.

It was a tough conversation and a long, cold walk home with the fall wind seeping through our sweaters.

I don't remember when that answer began to shift, or exactly what happened to cause the change. It was more of a slow realization about the language I was using to answer the question, and how language was forcing me into an inauthentic role. The question wasn't about becoming a parent again. I was already a parent. I became a parent when my first baby was born in 1993, and I would always be a parent, from that point on. I couldn't separate myself from the role. To pretend to not be a parent to a baby my partner was raising felt artificial and impossible.

So, I told her, sometime early in the winter, that I wanted to co-parent a baby with her. I had a lot of parent wisdom and skills to offer. I wanted to have a baby with her, a baby we would make and raise together. Yes, I was certain.

We needed to find some sperm.

The next set of conversations took place over email. One by one, we drafted long, awkward questions to the few people on our dear friend list who might have sperm they would consider offering us so we could make a baby. "Would you be at all willing to think about …?" "Could you imagine yourself open to the possibility of …?" "Would you be open to having conversations with us …?" We made it clear that we didn't want a father for our baby — we would be the parents — and we didn't want their role to be a secret. We would be explaining to this theoretical future baby at some point, likely pretty early in their childhood, that they had been made with the help of a very dear friend who gave us some sperm. And we said that the donor could choose their relationship to the baby, anywhere from good friend like any other to some kind of uncle figure who fits into the "unconditionally important family forever" category.

One by one, those lovely friends wrote loving, kind and thoughtful messages back to us. No, they couldn't. No, they wouldn't. One knew for certain that he couldn't not be Dad to a biological kid of his. One had just had a vasectomy after deciding that he and his partner would have only the one kid who was now three years old. One was too overwhelmed with his PhD dissertation and the search for a job in academia. The answers made us cry, and made us love our friends even more.

And then someone said yes. Enthusiastically, definitely, joyfully, *yes*.

We were living as part of a collective house where we shared two floors with three other adults, five cats and a dog. Maybe it sounds strange for a couple to ask a group of friends or roommates for permission to get pregnant, but we weren't just friends, and certainly much more than roommates. The five of us talked about each other as chosen family, and we felt a deep, loving, long-term commitment to sharing our lives. Deciding to have a baby required the consent, and for us the active participation of, the people we were making a home with — who we celebrated with, created with, grieved with. It felt like a huge ask, bigger than the sperm question. It was going to take some serious processing.

We had plenty of one-on-one conversations, and then on a Sunday in May we all sat down together to tackle the question: Could we have a baby? Twelve hours later — hours of talking, explaining, questioning, crying, listening, laughing and, of course, eating — we agreed we would wait for six months before trying. In those six months we'd all work on building a set of emotional conditions that would help the house be ready to welcome a baby. It felt a little like limbo, but it wasn't a no: just wait and work and we'll see how it feels after six months.

Our donor was dating one of our housemates. As part of our ongoing conversations about what the donor's role would be, the four of us sat down for dinner at the Nicaraguan restaurant around the corner from our house. I don't remember what I ordered, just the giddy excitement that was shooting through every nerve in my body. We all laughed a lot about the potential awkwardness of the baby's creation process. And then we started talking about what it would feel like if our donor and our housemate broke up. In the moment, the possibility seemed like one more theoretical future scenario, but it happened, before we had even one insemination try. Fortunately, they had both agreed that it wouldn't change their commitment to our project.

Watching a dear friend navigate a painful breakup can be challenging. Asking that friend's ex to come over to your shared house once a month to masturbate in the office next to her bedroom is next-level challenging. We wrote a lot of apologetic texts and made phone calls arranging timing so that our housemate could decide if she wanted to be in the house or not. We tried our best to check in with her to see if her commitment had waned. It hadn't. She was exceptionally honest, generous and forgiving, and her bravery is an important element in the birth stories we tell.

It took five months of trying, tracking morning temperatures, describing states of mucus, peeing on ovulation prediction sticks and waiting out the angsty days between the insemination and the answer. The first few times felt really sexy and romantic and exciting. Around January, it started to feel a bit mechanical. We agreed with our donor that we'd try for six months and then reassess.

My previous experience with getting pregnant and giving birth looked, and in many ways felt, pretty heteronormative. My former partner and I had decided not to have any kids, and then my only brother died of AIDS in the early nineties. I watched my parents suffer and I knew I had the capacity to do something healing and life-giving. So, we had a baby. And then, two years later, a second.

I carried both babies, birthed them vaginally and breastfed them. Their other parent had an intense full-time job with the provincial government, so I took on the role of stay-at-home mom and worked on writing projects and editing jobs on the side. I wrote my first novel before the younger kid was old enough to go to school.

My ex and I were both closeted queers — I had come out as bisexual in the late eighties but no one seemed to pay any attention since I was living with someone everyone assumed was a male partner. She didn't come out as trans until years later, after our kids were grown up and we'd decided to separate. We spent most of the years of their childhood passing as a straight family in a cute old house in a rural river valley in Nova Scotia.

Sometime in the spring, after the twelve-hour house meeting, I called the kids — both now in their twenties and supporting themselves in a different city — and told them what was happening. It's still in the idea stage, I told them. I shared our joke about theoretical future baby. They both seemed unsurprised: "It makes sense, Mom. Sure, do it. Let us know when it's a real thing."

That was the first of several conversations, each of which dug a little deeper into the questions, the feelings and their processing of the whole idea. One said he would be angry, later, if it seemed like this baby got a better childhood than he had. I told him I was grateful for his honesty, explained that it would be different, but not necessarily better. And if I do get better at being a parent, I told him, you'll benefit too.

The older one said he wasn't sure he wanted anyone but him and his brother to call me Mom. It's okay, I told him, I'm not sure I want that either. Saying it out loud crystallized the notion for me. I didn't want to be this baby's mother. Definitely their parent, not their mother.

I searched for titles, for words to call myself that felt linguistically and culturally appropriate and, most importantly, gender neutral. I'd been feeling more and more certain about identifying as being outside the gender binary, but definitely still on the tomboy end of the spectrum.

Eventually, what felt most comfortable and real was for the baby to call me Jo. Rachel would be their Mama and I would be their Jo. Secretly, I began a little hope that maybe the baby would have trouble with the J sound and end up calling me Do-Do. That would feel good, too, I decided. I started collecting dad jokes and wondering if I could live up to my own father's model of map-reading and knot-tying and fire-building skills. I'd need to work on my Boy Scout badges before this baby was ready to be born.

It was March, on the fifth attempt, when the pregnancy test was finally positive. Suddenly, theoretical future baby was real, growing and changing our lives already, even though they were still only the size of a poppy seed.

In late October, a little over a month before the due date, one of our friends hosted a party for us. She proposed a shower but the concept felt weird and inauthentic, so we came up with the notion of a "baby work party" — people came over and helped with tasks that would make welcoming the baby into the house a little easier. Some people worked together to make huge batches of food which they packaged up as two-person dinners and froze; another group sewed patches with phrases like "We will Not be Pacified" and "Boobs not Bombs" on tiny onesies and sleepers; and another group made two beautiful mobiles. My favourite is the one with clouds and rain-drops. I remember watching my adult kid sitting on our living room floor putting careful stitches in a pale blue felt raindrop.

In the middle of the party Rachel and I gathered everyone together to read them a series of commitments we had written to each other and to the baby. I promised her I would make loving space "for all our ideas and manifestations of family." She promised to nurture my "handsome, gentle, softball-star body" and my "poet heart." We committed not to shield the baby from the fucked-up-ness of this world, and to surround them with "people, stories and examples that show you how you can fight like hell to change it."

We wanted our friends and family — our community — to witness us. We wanted to be held accountable, to have people hear us say the words and support us in fulfilling those commitments.

I'm writing this now with a baby monitor sitting on the desk beside me. Our kiddo, S, has been out in the world for longer than they were growing inside Rachel. Upstairs in their hand-me-down crib, they're asleep in rocket ship pyjamas, the clouds and rain-drops of the homemade mobile spinning slowly over their head. Everywhere they look, there is evidence of the collection of people surrounding them, helping to raise them. We call them house-mates or loved ones or grandparents or siblings or friends. They are all family. They've all made a commitment to be part of S's life and help them flourish.

My commitments are already being tested, sometimes in the ways I expected and others in ways I couldn't have predicted with any certainty. I don't remember the last time I had an uninterrupted six-hour stretch of sleep. Both older kids tell me how life-affirming it is to hang out with S. Strangers assume I'm a grandmother way less often than I worried they would. When it happens, I just give S a squeeze, smile and say, "Nope, I'm a parent."

So much of this process, this adventure, has hinged on trying to find language for talking about what doesn't already have a name. I've been searching for ways to express, authentically and comfortably, the true significance and meaning of these life-changing roles, relationships and identities. In the coming years, as S learns to talk and express their questions, their wonderings, their feelings, we'll continue the language-seeking process and the telling and re-telling of how they came to be made. And I'll continue the journey of figuring out how to tell my own story of becoming.

How My Blended Family was Brought Together by Same Love

Beth McDonough

Last April, I went from a family of one to a family of four. I married my partner, Jen, and along with her came a brilliant, bold, beautiful five-year-old little girl. This child also brought with her another parent, my wife's ex and my stepdaughter's other mother. That's right; we're a three-mom family, full of estrogen and energy, and we four have learned to navigate this world as a team, because there's enough working against us already. We're here, we're queer and we have enough maternal instinct to raise a whole softball team.

My stepdaughter, Mia, sparked the creation of our unconventional family by finding her two Moms through private adoption. Mia knows her own birth story well thanks to an open dialogue encouraged by Jamie Lee Curtis's children's book *Tell Me Again About the Night I Was Born*. Although this story evolves as she matures and thinks of new questions to ask and depths to explore, Mia has no question of how hard her parents worked to be in her life.

Mia happily informs her classmates that she grew big and strong inside the belly of a kind, hard-working woman (let's call her Nina) who kept her safe until her forever parents came to take her home. Although her first year of preschool included some awkward conversations with other parents whose children Mia had convinced that every baby grows in Nina's belly before finding his or her parents, the strategy of candid and open honesty has paid off over the years. Hopefully Mia's anecdote has given those families a whole new option for the response to the age-old question, *Where do babies come from?*

The grown-up version of Mia's story is no less sweet and inspirational, just with a few added adult layers. Jen and her ex-partner learned of Mia's swiftly approaching entrance into this world about eight weeks before she was born, from a friend of a family member. The biological mother was a young Iraqi refugee living in Arizona, with dark hair, deep-set eyes and a hunger for the freedom to be a woman in America able to pursue an education without fear of persecution.

Nina enrolled in a university and began taking classes and steps toward reaching the full potential that was unavailable to her in her home country. As her twenty-first birthday approached, she was taken out by some friends to celebrate the American, college-student way. Naïve to the effects of excessive alcohol consumption and innocent of the consequences that can arise from unprotected sexual encounters, Nina continued living her life after her birthday came and went, unaware that my soon-to-be step-daughter was getting big and strong inside her belly.

About seven months post-celebration, Nina went to the doctor and learned not only that she was pregnant, but also that she was just two short months away from giving birth. Only then did Nina become aware that a tiny life was growing inside her, and friends in America had to explain how that could have happened and what her options were. Adamant to pursue her educational aspirations — the primary reason she'd fled to America — and determined to find a safe space for this baby she didn't quite comprehend how she'd made, Nina decided to keep the baby and began to privately search for a loving family whose home and life were ready to raise a child.

As the birthdate quickly approached, Nina had to make a decision between three different couples who wanted the opportunity to raise her beautiful baby as their own. Jen and her partner were wrought with dread over being passed over for cookie-cutter straight couples, equipped to provide this child with the traditional, heterosexual and white-picket-fence life that so many adoption agencies both within and outside of the US still prefer.

To their surprise, though, Nina had already made up her mind.

In Iraq, men aren't exactly known for their flawless treatment of women. Murder, rape and burning are just some of the words that come to mind in relation to the fears women face daily from men in Iraq. Because freedom from this type of male-dominated persecution was the primary reason Nina had fled the country, she was drawn to my wife and her partner as an all-female environment for the nurturing of her unborn daughter.

Eight short weeks later, Mia arrived. Nina selflessly let her forever Mommies cut the cord, giving both herself and her biological daughter a future of opportunities neither of them would have known otherwise. Mia experienced her first plane ride at just a few days old, journeying from Arizona back to Pennsylvania, where she would be surrounded by love every moment of every day.

I feel like I've known Mia all of her life, but I first met her after she'd been in this world for three years, with her Shirley Temple red hair and those same deep-set eyes I've seen in her biological mother's photos. I fell in love with her in an instant, and every day I wake up grateful to be one of the Mommies the universe has chosen to be part of this little girl's life. This fiery, fiercely independent child who, on a spiritual level, has picked me to help shape her into someone who is going to make this world a better place.

Jen and I married in April of last year, and our ceremony included a gift and a promise to Mia that I will work hard every hour of every day to be the presence in her life that she deserves. As her third mom, the purpose of that presence isn't always completely clear, but who says we're all expected to have the answers all the time?

My parenting role isn't that of the traditional blended family, which is more of a blessing than a burden. I remember my mother scrambling to fill the Mom role in my own blended family, carving out the time to pack my stepbrother's lunch and conducting most of the discipline while his dad worked ungodly hours. In turn, we all became accustomed to just sliding into heteronormative gender roles right where they had been left after Mom and my stepdad divorced.

As for this family I have created for myself, we have no gender roles because we're all women. If I notice the lunch hasn't been packed, I pack it. Whoever starts one avenue of discipline is the one who carries it through. Notice the trash is full? Take it out. We're all moms in this house, so no spot is vacant and needs to be filled, because my wife and I are both the mommy and the daddy, if you please.

The dynamics of our queer blended family actually make for a smoother, co-parenting experience than most might think. Mia's other mom (or Mama, as she calls her) has never lashed out for fear of her role in Mia's life being threatened by a new parent, because we're all moms here. I'm not filling a spot left empty in this house, but rather adding more love to a little girl's life whose cup is already full. So why not continue to pour into this cup to run it over? Better yet, let's trade the cup in for a pitcher, and then when it's full, she can pour some into the next cup, and the next one after that.

The beginning stages of navigating a new blended family and the roles that go along with it are never easy, but I'm a firm believer that women's maternal instincts kick into high gear here. Each one of us puts Mia's needs first, and she's thriving because of it. She started soccer this year, and Mommy (my wife) is the coach. So, on any given Saturday, you can find Mama and me on the sideline beside each other, both of us with a pompom in one hand and a camera in the other, cheering on both Mia and Mommy.

In fact, Mia loves having a plethora of Mommies so much that she is determined to get another one into the picture. Mia's Mama is bisexual, like me, and her last serious relationship was with a man, whom she dated for two of the last three years. Since they separated, Mia has announced on multiple occasions that she would prefer Mama to have a girl partner because she would rather have four Mommies than three Mommies and one Daddy. I was recently in my friend's wedding, and afterward, Mia scoffed at the fact that this wedding now meant my friend was married to her boyfriend and was no longer available to marry Mama and become her fourth Mom. The concept of polygamy is another explanation for another day, after all.

Because we defy gender roles in both of Mia's houses, colours like blue and pink don't define masculinity and femininity. Dresses aren't limited to girls, and taking the trash out isn't a boy's job. All my stepdaughter knows is that everyone who needs more love should get to feel more love, regardless of gender, birthplace, age, status or anything in between. Aside from her new-found role as matchmaker, our bright-eyed first grader has informed both of her best friends (a boy and a girl) in class that only one of them can be more than just her friend. My wife and I celebrate this statement as an indication that we've done our job, all while we consider re-moving the nails that attach her bedroom door to the wall, because apparently her love triangles are starting early, but we'll be damned if they start at six years old.

As my wife and I begin to get more serious about growing our family, I can't help but reflect on how serendipitous the birth of it has been. Mommy and Mama discovered Nina at just the right time, in the right place, and they were just the right people to raise a little girl Nina would want to see grow up to smash glass ceilings and shatter the patriarchy. As Nina goes on to achieve her dreams, room is made for me to join these women in adding what I have to offer, to expand this caring, queer, unconventional family by one, to add more love. Now we wonder how organically we will continue to grow. Will it be twins? Will another fearless female join our ranks? Will we finally add some testosterone to this gang of girl power? However the chips fall, I know I've hit the jackpot with my blended, same-love family. If you ever meet us, I promise that each one of us will do our best to make you feel more love. And to all of my step- (better yet, bonus) Mommies out there, you always have a role, a need to be met and a cup to overflow.

Baby Dinosaur

Nicola Harwood

I come across the eviscerated baby dinosaur this morning as I walk the children to school. It is their first day back since the massacre in Connecticut. The eight-year-old is crying. She has just fallen down. The eleven-year-old is fussing and apologizing as she likely caused the younger one to trip.

Let nothing disturb thee, let nothing dismay thee.

We're walking along, the younger one sniffling and the older one fussing, and there it is: flat on its back, belly exposed, legs spread, arms spread, tiny skull looking left. The skin is white, damp and cold. It folds like human skin — at the elbow, at the knee. At first I think it might be a dead lizard, dropped from the sky by a distracted eagle. But we don't have lizards this far north. This baby dinosaur thing is about seven inches long. Its tail runs out between its legs, curving slightly away from the body.

Lately the children have been counting porta-potties. The blue portable toilets attendant at most construction sites around the city. At last count they had breached two hundred. The older one keeps track of the numbers. She has a mind like a steel trap. The younger one made a leap yesterday, saw the orange storm fencing around a house about to be demolished and shouted, "Two hundred and six!" But the eleven-year-old isn't buying it: "You have to see it. You can't just count anything."

Usually I make them walk ahead of me because they talk incessantly and I am easily bored. Today I am clutching the youngest as she recovers from the pain of falling and pushing the older one to go ahead. On Friday when I picked them up from school I held both of their hands all the way home. I don't think they have heard about the killings. We don't watch much TV. I don't really want them to know. Though a few weeks ago the youngest one told me her class was practising hiding in a cupboard and being quiet in case an intruder came into the school. They call this Code Red.

"Awesome!" says the older one, who is generally fearless. The baby dinosaur has had its stomach and brains eaten out. Other than that, it's in pretty good shape, for whatever it is. Which is sort of bugging me. Amateur wildlife watcher, I can usually at least determine the species of most animals we come across, living or dead. But this thing lying on the sidewalk in a suburban street of Vancouver is a mystery. Is it an escaped albino pet lizard caught by the neighbour's cat who chewed its guts out then abandoned it? The prize carrion from some wayward desert owl who carried it north from Palm Springs?

I haven't known these children for very long. I moved in with them and their mother a year ago. When I was their age the only emergency preparedness we did at school was a fire drill once or twice a year. Hiding in a cupboard and being silent? Jesus Christ.

I have my own son who is thirty-two years old. His childhood traumas were few. He was once attacked by a rooster and once abandoned by his mother. That's me.

I have a semi-frequent obsession with a couple I know who lost their twelve-year-old daughter in a house fire. Months before the fire I had heard the mother announce publicly how raising her daughter was her proudest accomplishment.

Let nothing disturb thee, let nothing dismay thee.

I left my son with his father and expected them to take care of themselves. Now I am back in the parenting saddle with my girlfriend's two children in tow through the relentless rain of a Vancouver winter, through wary explanations of school massacres, through the poking of eviscerated dinosaurs with sticks.

"Take a picture and send it to Mama!" the oldest one commands.

Now I think perhaps it is an aborted raccoon. It has long fingers and toes. But no fur. At what point in the embryonic stage of a raccoon's prenatal development does it grow the ringed tale, the masked robber eyes?

Last week I read about a young woman who eviscerated the family dog while it was still alive then posted pictures of it on the internet. Apparently once the police searched her dorm room and found weapons, charged her with cruelty to animals and she served a few months in jail, they had to release her. She has admitted to obsessing about killing a homeless person and also, at one point, obsessing about killing her drunk college roommate. She landed in this world like some wild thing dropped from above, on all fours, ready to attack. But there is not much the authorities can do.

Children threaten disaster at every turn, they spin out into the universe and sometimes don't return. At least not in any recognizable form.

My fingers are numb from the cold as I snap the picture on my phone. I want to be numb when I see the newspaper photos of families gathered around candles and teddy bears. But I am so angry. Fuck it. Fuck them. Fuck them all.

Let nothing disturb thee, let nothing dismay thee.

If you asked my thirty-two-year-old son if he's angry with his mother for abandoning him when he was two, he will likely smile, bemused, and shrug. He keeps his cards close to his chest. I invite him and his wife to dinner. I have returned in another form. I study the bone structure in his face; the sense of humour; the wariness.

My worst nightmare of motherhood is feeling nothing at all.

The bullets that the gunman (or gun-child — he was only twenty) used explode inside you. All three of the gunman's weapons were owned and registered in his mother's name. He shot her first.

Let nothing disturb thee, let nothing dismay thee.

Children explode inside you. Penetrate your vital organs: slivers of metal shattering the heart, the lungs, the liver, the spleen.

Remember that we are dust and wind and shadow.

I'm not even sure who I want to fuck themselves or to get fucked. The media? The gunman? The innocent families? Does the fact that they are American and participate in America make them suspect? But when I read the timeline of deadly school shootings, I discover that mass shootings are not just an American thing. They have happened in Germany and in Russia, in Finland, Brazil and Canada. In fact, we Canadians have three school shootings to our credit.

Connecticut is billed as the "second deadliest school shooting in history." So now these things have a history. They are part of the culture. Children practising hiding in cupboards and staying silent has become a school routine.

The thing is there again this afternoon when I walk to pick the children up. I take more photos. It is strangely human — the damp white skin, the muscles in the arms, the elbow joint, the shoulder, the leg. I snap and snap then pull myself away. It's almost 3 p.m. I arrive at the school with many other parents hovering around the entrance. The kids still don't seem to have any knowledge of the massacre.

"Nobody believed me when I told them what we saw on the way to school!"

"It's still there."

"Can we see it again?"

Once they arrive in your house, by whatever means, they're yours. There are only so many rules. You show up. You put in time. Don't drop things from large heights. Pay attention. All you really need to do is pay attention.

Dust and wind and shadow.

We retrace our route back and on the way we come across a second body. This one has grey fur and a long tail and I identify it pretty much immediately as a rat. It is also missing its guts and what is left of its head is squished into the mud and grass.

I feel a little sick when I realize.

The white, furless one is probably a rat. The long hands and feet. The shape of the skull. The teeth. I don't know why it makes me feel sick, but it does. We continue on until we come to it. Children stream by on their way home from school. I hold the hands of the two girls. We stare at the white, hairless body for a long time.

I thought this eviscerated baby dinosaur was something interesting, even exotic. Something special. But it's not.

THE BOY IN ME

Natalie Meisner

Gentle reader, I have a confession to make: There is a boy in me and he's always been there. I knew this long before my wife and I decided to try and become pregnant; long before we found out that I was in fact pregnant with a flesh-and-blood son, our infant boy; long before we found out that she, too, only two months later, was pregnant with our second son and that we were *Double Pregnant*[1] and soon-to-be mothers to two exuberant and unique boys who would rock and forever alter our lives — for the chaotic and the better.

I knew there was a boy in me as my body hurled through space and surged from root to leaf tip of the biggest sugar maple in my grandmother's back field. As I hacked at green wood to draw the sap with my very own jackknife. I knew it as I scaled a sheer rock face and *bloody knee be damned*. At the top of the rock we sat, the boy and I, and licked off the sweet blood that gathered there. *Who cares about a cut, we did it!* The boy in me chaffed and shucked off scratchy lace dresses; blasted off down the road leaving in the dust adult voices telling us to:

slow down
be careful
act like a lady
put a shirt on

---

1. *Double Pregnant: Two Lesbians Make a Family* (Fernwood, 2014) is a full-length work of creative non-fiction that charts the journey of my wife and me as we, a bi-racial and bi-national lesbian couple, looked for and eventually found a known donor to help us start a family. We go through pregnancy together and deliver our two sons just eight weeks apart. It spent time on Canadian non-fiction bestseller charts, was a finalist for the Atlantic Book Awards and was the foundation for a stage play, *Speed Dating For Sperm Donors*, that debuted at Lunchbox Theatre in Calgary and Neptune Theatre in Halifax.

Can you imagine how he felt, gentle reader? The boy in me, how he roared approval as we plunged our hands in the sweet, sweet dirt just to feel the living twist of worms? As I squared off with the bully down the road to feel the good crunch of his fist on my cheekbone and the connection as my knuckles met his. We were sorting it out and would be friends afterward. The boy in me knew this without a doubt.

As I handed a mangled flower to the first pretty girl whose smile made my guts twist, the boy in me nearly died from shame, but his hand was right there, in mine. Slightly grubby and scuffed, strong from swinging the monkey bars.

Of course, I know now that none of those things are *boy* any more than placing gentle lips on a feverish forehead or rocking a beloved to sleep are *girl*. Strength and gender are fluid and course through us in ebbs and flows like blood, but this is a lesson we all have to learn: trying to stop the flow is like trying to stop the tide from brimming in over the flat shimmer of sand at the sea shore.

It was hard to know it then, however. In the small fishing village where I grew up, baiting a hook, learning to tie knots and hurling my body down a ravine — the things that gave me joy — seemed hard coded to boyishness. When my boy friends rough-and-tumbled it, people would ruffle their hair and shake their heads. When I did it, the acrid taste of scorn seeped from adults toward me. When my friends tackled and tussled and duked it out, their dads would scold them outwardly but inside gleamed a rich streak of silent approval: *He's standing up for himself.* When I did it, it wasn't right: uncouth, unnatural, savage.

The boy in me knew what he needed, however, and he egged me on past raised eyebrows and insults and policies that would hold me down. *Go, go, go,* he'd chant, and I'd surge on, never minding pain nor broken bones nor even common sense. There were times we went too far, trying to prove it didn't hurt, and it's lucky that torn ligaments, scars and forever tender spots are the only souvenirs of these times.

Once the boy in me and I applied for the most adventurous job imaginable: you are dropped from a bush plane in the Canadian north with a map and everything you need to survive in a backpack. You walk for twelve-hour stretches over solitary places where perhaps only bears and wolves have walked before. Every few kilometres, you take soil samples and at night you pitch camp, make dinner and sleep in a one-person tent under the stars. As I handed in my resume and explained why I was fit for the job, the boy in me thrummed with excitement. He was already figuring out how to use the bear bangers and the best ways to pitch camp. But the man behind the desk was the first in a series of men behind desks to hold up his hand and try to drive a wedge between my boy and me.

"Can you cook at all?" the man asked, willing to hire me to splash bland chilli onto plates for the men who go out to do the work.

"I can't send a woman out to the bush. Bears are attracted to the smell of blood. When you get your period they'll come after you," he stated in bold contravention of scientific fact, but with an eerie confidence in his absurd statement. The boy in me hooted with laughter, but on the outside, my face lit with rage. Time had taught me that I could no longer throw punches and that the sting of tears would not help, either. So instead, my boy and me, we swallowed hard. He's been my constant companion and 3 a.m. conspirator through decades of an improvised, fly-by-the-seat-of-your-pants life — frequently getting me trouble, but then out of it, too.

So how to describe, then, the gush of electric excitement when the exquisite ultrasound technician — a goth with blue-black hair, eyebrow studs and wizardly eyes — waved the techno-magic wand over my barely protruding belly and uttered the following like a sacred incantation: "You've got a boy in there."

The words reached inside like a multivalent key and unlocked rooms and chambers of feelings I didn't know existed. Having a child challenges everything we think we know about the self, about subjectivity and about ownership. The child is yours in responsibility and yet not yours to keep. I used to think children come out as a kind of blank slate, but this is not so. Each infant emerges and fixes upon their loved ones a singular gaze and a unique intelligence in molten form. The job of parenting from this perspective can seem like that of a very invested guide, or (later on, when you are carrying their gear) even a Sherpa as they scale their own Mount Everests.

The technician, waving her magic wand, had made manifest, made flesh, the secret of my life: *There is a boy inside me.*

Who will be caught in my wife's strong and loving hands and fulfil her dearest wish? Her son, my son, his own self.

And another, in my wife's belly —

Who I, in turn, will catch. And as our two sons — not twins but something like it — make the arduous crossing from their idyllic aquatic world to this one, there is terror. How will we protect them from all the hard edges, literal and figurative? Coffee table edges, concrete curbs, thorns and sharp sticks wait to snag them, I am sure. But what about playground words, hate speech, boxes on forms and casual jabs from thoughtless adults? At the thought of any harm coming to a single hair, to a tiny moon toenail of our babies, a savage strength curls up like smoke from my core. During labour, I feel primordial sabre-tooth mama's fangs burst through my gums. When I have a chance to look in the mirror days later, I am shocked to see they have receded. It must be safe now.

How did we get to this place? Two dykes, two mothers of two almost-twins? Gentle reader, you may certainly be asking yourselves this right now, and fairly so. Of course, we did not have the option of suspending birth control and letting nature take its course. What we actually did was walk out into a blizzard on the Canadian Prairies nine years ago and confess to one another a secret wish to have children of our own. Then we walked down the street, hand in hand, blissed out as if inside some exquisitely constructed queer Canadian snow globe. We had no idea that night of the two-year, multi-country saga that would become our search for the Mr. Right known donor. We had no idea at that time of the heartbreak we'd experience when a potential donor changed his mind. No idea of the logistics involved with fertility treatments and follicle counts and donor agreements. We were as yet innocent to the passports and official documents (not to mention government officials) we would have to confront that insist a family only has slots for one mother and one father. We couldn't know then how badly this would sting and how hard we would have to fight to have a simple box changed, even when the law was on our side.

Yet we could not be daunted by stones on the path. We will not give up. Not then, not now. While there has been much written about mothers and mothering (still not yet enough from a kind perspective, but that is a matter for another time), I am not sure that I have seen, in life or on the page, the kind of mother my wife has become. The way she relates to children is a thing of quiet beauty. Out on the sports pitch or in the workshop as she shows them the proper grip for a power tool, or as they stand together discussing the best way to solve a problem, all the stultifying laws of gender seem to suspend themselves for a moment and quiver. My wife is a woman of colour standing over six feet tall with a commanding yet gentle presence. A woman who treats tasks most of us can only dream of — weld metal, fly a solo airplane, draw up blueprints for a new kind of machine — as a matter of course. A woman to whom you can confidently toss the keys to anything but whose touch as she holds a child is as tender as any on earth. A woman who, just by existing, causes us to widen our notions of what is woman. What *is* woman? What is man? What is a mother or a father? The boy in me seemed to know how to hold a baby without dropping him. He never considered looking after children beneath him and he leapt at the chance to play. To just play all day long, which is what babies crave from us most. Even more than milk.

So then imagine how we must have felt when we went together for a second ultrasound to find out that we had not one, but two sons on the way. This time, the magic wand revealed the outline of an exquisite boy so tender and perfect, a beautiful leaf unfolding. He was the new shoot of two continents and several storied bloodlines.

Another little boy who is both ours and his own self. Who will hear the stories we have to tell and make his own bold imprint, emblazoned on us.

As we lie together at night, our bodies curl against one another as two new beings foment inside us. We feel four hearts beating and wonder at the beauty and strangeness of the world. Two mothers; two sons born to a bi-racial, bi-national family. A kind of symmetry seems to be taking root in our otherwise offbeat life and we await it happily through a snow-globe winter on the Canadian Prairies.

Which isn't to say that we are without worry. Although some women report feeling wonderful during pregnancy, invigorated and blissful and embracing the "glow" that strangers determinedly notice in you once you become visibly pregnant, this was not my experience. The body that my boy and I had shared, had spent decades challenging, pushing to the limits of endurance, suddenly changed shape with such speed and single mindedness that we were horrified. It became heavy and sodden, awkward and weak.

Why are we sitting ducks at the time fierceness is most called for?
Why are our brains foggy when we most need to be sharp?

We raged and shrank away from the weakness, from the pins and needles in arms and legs. The size of the baby inside and the size of his gateway to this world (a.k.a., my vagina) were clearly at odds. What could this be but a kind of design flaw? A genetic *whoops?*

I wondered why other women told the terrifying stories of their labour with quivering excitement and relish. The gorier and more hair-raising, the more they seemed to languish in the detail, to work on their pacing and delivery — just really savour and enjoy the telling: *Three days in labour, no pain meds. When the baby finally came I was all torn apart down there. Nothing left but some flaps of skin like tattered curtains …*

The boy in me frantically crushes his hands over his ears and I'm with him. The only reason I can think for telling these stories with such gusto is the same reason soldiers tell battles of the front:

We came back, we survived. Here, see the scars and shattered bones.

And yet birthing brings us into the world while battles take us out. The boy and I find this to be such a paradox that we let it lie.

Other physical changes are also alarming, most notably the breasts that suddenly spilled over my sports bra, jutting out in front and preceding me when I entered a room. I know that on other women these new breasts would be exquisitely beautiful. Something for Rodin or Camille Claudel to chisel from stone. Other women would simply buy a V-neck sweater and enjoy the ride. The boy in me had moments of appreciation. If such a thing were possible, he might have cat-called himself. On a logical plane, I understand the satisfaction that women derive from feeding their child from their body and it makes sense. But at the same time, the idea that milk would soon flow from my body was horrifying. I was wakened by feverish dreams of being chased by red-eyed bovines — but the bovine was me. When the moment came, however, the horror faded and I made my peace with the process. The breasts filled with milk at the rate that our son needed to drink. I appreciated the functionality but coped by imagining the breasts as free-floating instruments, arriving and docking at portals each time the baby needed to drink. The action hero straps on her equipment and is grateful when it works as needed. When the breasts were no longer needed and receded to the familiar bumps that have lived on my body since adolescence, the boy and I were relieved.

The physical fears and challenges of being mothers to sons in this world, in this culture, I do not think we have shrunk from. Not my wife nor I, nor the boy in me who even learned to hold his nose and change diapers ripe enough to send anyone screaming. We all, mothers and sons, the boy in me and the girl in you, have to figure it out and show up every day and bring our best to the table. We all enlarge what it means to mother, to father, to nurture and to parent, and this is for the best.

But there are other dimensions of shimmying this far out on a branch, of mothering a son in this world. Sometimes the boy in me goes rogue. Whispers harshly the jagged schoolyard insults he learned so long ago. He gets mad. At me, at the world, at me. Like a boomerang: *It's not fair! It's a raw deal!* But what if our boys drank this anger in our milk? What if they are swayed by the voices of generations of grinding conformity? What if our beloved boys shoot up suddenly to man size one day and ask, Where's my father? Why did you bring me into this world with no father?

And this is pain that transcends the physical. What if no matter how much love and care and strength we bring to being their parents, no matter how tenderly we hold them then learn to let them go, no matter how many bad dreams we chase away, how many hours spent listening and soccer matches cheered for — beyond the years of laughter and scars, accrued boo-boos kissed and warm laughter around the family dinner table — what if our sons lift their heads one day and tell us, You aren't good enough.

That is a white-hot burn. But as I write, I realize this fear is not unique to us as two mothers. It is the fear of every parent, and for good reason.

Maybe I am not good enough is a thought that must have crossed every parent's mind at the end of a feverish night with an infant; in the moment where you just can't make it better and all you can do is sit and rock and wait for first light or the fever to break. And yet this feeling isn't stitched to our heels: it is just a phantom that becomes as spooky as we let it. And with this thought, gentle reader, may all your fears and worries be released like a big breath out at the end of a long run.

As the boy in me holds the girl in you with all the tenderness of an infant's gaze.

ACKNOWLEDGEMENTS

My deepest thanks to the contributors, who candidly and courageously shared their intimate, heartfelt family stories; this collection would not exist without you.

Thanks to my publisher, Vici Johnstone, for not only championing this anthology but also contributing her story. Thanks also to the rest of the team at Dagger Editions/Caitlin Press, especially Holly Vestad and Michael Despotovic, for making the birth of this book such a smooth experience.

Thanks to Beth Duncan, Allison Campbell and the gang at Pomegranate Community Midwives in East Vancouver, whose Twats and Tots LGBTQ2+ parenting speaker series planted the early seeds for this book.

Thanks to Rachel Rose for the best "welcome baby" gift ever, a copy of *Between Interruptions: 30 Women Tell the Truth About Motherhood* (editor Cori Howard, Key Porter Books, 2007). Your beautiful, eloquent essay, "A Tale of Two Mommies," confirmed my desire to create this anthology.

Thanks to Cori Howard and the Momoir Project for providing mentoring, community and a place to steal away and write while my son was still tiny — it was here that I drafted the initial proposal for what would become *Swelling with Pride*. Thanks also to my Momoir cohort who went on to form Write Club ("The first rule of Write Club is: you do not talk about Write Club.") — Jane Swinglehurst, Liesl Jurock, Megan Frazer, Tanya Hansen, Jill Imrie and Maia Gibb. I am grateful for your unwavering friendship and encouragement through this book's long gestation.

Thanks to my students (past and present) and my colleagues at the University of British Columbia Creative Writing Program. To Lauren Turner, my literary cousin and comrade-in-arms. To Stephanie Bolster, Maureen McEvoy and Emilie Elizabeth

Klaussen, who offered cheerleading and support at critical junctures in this book's development. To Yung Adetiba for the lovely author photo.

And last but not least, thanks to my beloved Amanda and Aidan. This collection would not exist without you, either.

ABOUT THE EDITOR

Sara Graefe is an award-winning playwright and screenwriter. As former publications coordinator for the Society of Special Needs Adoptive Parents, she authored the bestselling special needs parenting book *Living with FASD: A Guide for Parents* and she edited the *Adoption Piece by Piece* trilogy (Groundwork Press). In 2007, she became a proud queer mom and began chronicling her experiences on her blog, Gay Girls Make Great Moms (queermommy. wordpress.com). Her creative non-fiction has appeared in various magazines and anthologies, including *Literary Mama, Walk Myself Home, Boobs: Women Explore What It Means to Have Breasts, Mothers and Sons, Telling Truths: Storying Motherhood* and *A Family By Any Other Name* (finalist for a 2015 Lambda Literary Award). She lives with her wife and school-aged son in Vancouver, on the unceded traditional territory of the Musqueam, Squamish and Tsleil-Waututh First Nations, and is on faculty in the Creative Writing Program at the University of British Columbia. For more information, visit saragraefe.com.

CONTRIBUTORS

andrea bennett's writing has been published by the *Atlantic, The Globe and Mail*, the *Walrus, Maisonneuve, Hazlitt, Reader's Digest* and others. Her essay "Water Upon the Earth" received gold in the essays category at the National Magazine Awards; her piece "Unmasked: Searching for lessons in Toronto's 2010 G20 debacle" received an **NMA** honourable mention in the politics and public interest category. andrea's first book of poetry, *Canoodlers*, came out with Nightwood Editions in 2014. Her travel guides to Montreal and Quebec City are forthcoming from Moon Travel.

Marusya Bociurkiw is the director of ten films and author of six books and over seventy-five scholarly, popular and arts-based articles. Her books have won and been shortlisted for several awards, including the Kobzar Award, Lambda Literary Award and Independent Publisher Award. She is an associate professor and director of the Studio for Media Activism & Critical Thought at Ryerson University in Toronto. Her most recent book, *Food Was Her Country: The Memoir of a Queer Daughter* (2018), is published by Caitlin Press.

Josephine Boxwell is a freelance writer and media specialist. Her short fiction and creative non-fiction have appeared in several publications, including the Caitlin Press anthology *Wherever I Find Myself: Stories by Canadian Immigrant Women* (2017). Originally from the **UK**, she now lives in **BC** with her partner and their two-year-old son.

Nicole Breit is an award-winning writer and online creative writing instructor. She lives in Gibsons, **BC**, on the traditional territory of the Sḵwx̱wú7mesh people, with her wife and two children. Her lyric essay "Spectrum," about life in a rainbow family, won the 2016 carte blanche / **CNFC** award, the same year she won *Room* magazine's creative non-fiction contest for "An Atmospheric Pressure." Nicole's work has appeared in *Hippocampus Magazine, Room* magazine, *Event, carte blanche* and the *Puritan*. nicolebreit.com.

Nelson, **BC**, poet **Jane Byers** "came out" with her second poetry collection, *Acquired Community*, in 2016 (Caitlin Press/Dagger Editions). It is a 2017 Goldie award winner for poetry and is featured on All Lit Up's Top Ten Social Justice Publications in Canada. Her debut poetry collection, *Steeling Effects*, is also published by Caitlin Press (2014). She has had poems and essays published in literary journals in Canada, the **US** and England, including in *The Best Canadian Poetry in English 2014*. She is the 2018 Writer-in-Residence for Simon Fraser University's ALOT Archives.

Susan G. Cole is a writer, editor and activist. She is the author of two books on violence against women, *Pornography and the Sex Crisis* (Second Story Press, 1993) and *Power Surge: Sex, Violence and Pornography* (Second Story Press, 1995) and is the editor of *Outspoken: Scenes and Monologues from Canadian Lesbian Plays* (Playwrights Canada Press, 2009). Her play, the comedy *A Fertile Imagination*, about two lesbians trying to have a baby, was nominated for two Dora Awards in Toronto. She lives in Toronto, where she is a political commentator and Books Editor at *NOW Magazine*, with her partner and has just become a grandmother.

Caitlin Crawshaw is an award-winning essayist and freelance journalist in Edmonton, and she holds an MFA in Creative Writing from UBC. Her writing credits include *Maclean's* and *Reader's Digest*, the literary journals *carte blanche* and *Plenitude*, and the anthology *The Remedy: Queer and Trans Voices on Health and Health Care* (Arsenal Pulp, 2016).

Emily Cummins-Woods is a registered social worker specializing in work with youth at risk. She brings an innovative and creative spirit to her facilitation and project coordination and has a passion for and background in dance, film and writing. Born and raised in Montreal, she currently lives with her partner and children in Kingston, Ontario.

Rachel Epstein is a long-time LGBTQ+ parenting activist, educator and researcher, and has written on a wide range of issues, including assisted human reproduction, queer spawn in schools, butch pregnancy, adoption and the tensions between queer sexuality, radicalism and parenting. From 2015–17 she was a Banting post-doctoral fellow at Brock University, conducting research on LGBTQ+ family conflict. She is currently the executive director of the United Jewish People's Order, a secular social justice organization.

Nicola Harwood is an Anglo-Canadian writer and interdisciplinary artist. Her work engages in community-based transformative processes and is often created in collaboration with other artists. Her writing has been published in various journals and her plays produced in Canada and the US. In 2016, Caitlin Press, in the launch of its imprint Dagger Editions, published her memoir about queer parenting, *Flight Instructions for the Commitment Impaired*. She teaches creative writing and interdisciplinary arts at Kwantlen Polytechnic University.

Terrie Hamazaki has performed her work at the Vancouver Fringe and Women in View performing arts festivals. Her writing has appeared in *Beyond the Pale: Dramatic Writing from First Nations Writers and Writers of Colour* (Playwrights Canada Press, 2004), *The Fed Anthology: Brand New*

Fiction and Poetry from the Federation of BC Writers (Anvil Press, 2003) and *Sustenance: Writers from BC and Beyond on the Subject of Food* (Anvil Press, 2017), among others. She works in the anti-violence against women sector.

Jo Jefferson is a Toronto-based queer writer and parent who grew up in Nova Scotia. Their poetry and short fiction have been published in *The Antigonish Review* and various anthologies, and their first novel, *Lightning and Blackberries*, was released by Nimbus Publishing in 2008. When they're not writing or reading, Jo hangs out with their toddler, works at a community centre, explores the world and facilitates workshops with curious creators of all ages.

Vici Johnstone has worked in theatre, radio, television, film and digital media. She was hired by Harbour Publishing as their production manager, and later the managing editor and general manager. She purchased Caitlin Press in 2008. Since that time, she has published dozens of titles, and in 2015, edited *This Place a Stranger: Canadian Women Travelling Alone.*

Patrice Leung is a Trinidad-born, Canadian-documented, lesbian single mother who wears glasses and is of Chinese descent, with a hint of Spanish sang-froid. Thank you for asking.

Eamon MacDonald enjoys long walks with dogs, playing music, reading books, knitting, quilting and baking pies, all while working as a researcher, educator and political theorist in Kingston, Ontario.

Janet Madsen was born on Canada's West Coast and has lived in various points in central Canada as well. She works in HIV education and advocacy; she and partner Tracy live with two teens in Vancouver.

Dr. Corinne L. Mason is a feminist killjoy academic and queer parent. She works as an associate professor of Gender and Women's Studies and Sociology at Brandon University, where she researches global LGBTQ rights, sexualized violence and reproductive justice. Mason has recently begun to publish creative non-fiction on the topics of queer pregnancy, loss and parenting. She lives in Winnipeg. corrinelmason.com.

Beth McDonough is a full-time bisexual and part-time freelance writer originally from the rolling hills of West Virginia. She currently lives with her brilliant wife and spunky stepdaughter in northwestern Pennsylvania, where she spends most of her time scouring books and television for LGBTQ representation and shouting into the abyss of the internet over the lack of it. You can follow her journey on her blog, The Babbling Blonde, or on Twitter (@bmacduhnuh).

Natalie Meisner's memoir *Double Pregnant: Two Lesbians Make a Family* was a finalist in the Atlantic Book Awards. Her play *Speed Dating For Sperm Donors* was a hit at Lunchbox and Neptune theatres and will be published by

Playwrights Canada Press in 2019. *Legislating Love: The Everett Klippert Story* recently debuted at Sage Theatre; her first book for children, *My Mommy, My Mama, My Brother and Me* is forthcoming from Nimbus. Natalie is a Professor in the Department of English at Mount Royal University in the areas of creative writing, drama and gender/sexuality studies. nataliemeisner.com

Susan Meyers is a mother, psychologist and runner from Kingston, Ontario. She loves tackling many things — going to school, being political, treating traumatized kids, teaching, gardening, running some slow marathons and learning to be a calmer and better person. Her hardest and most rewarding endeavour is being a mom.

Kira Meyers-Guiden is passionate about creating queer theatre that is representative of her community. Her works have been performed at festivals such as **IMPACT**, Gay Play Day and OutFest. She is an alumna of The Women's Room, an all-female playwriting unit (Sounderlust and Pat the Dog Theatre Creation). She is pursuing her master's degree at York University's Theatre & Performance Studies program. Her one-person show, *Queer Spawn*, is in development with Pat the Dog with plans on touring in early 2019.

Heather Osborne's writing explores queer relationships and gender identity through science fiction and fantasy, and she is an associate editor for *Foundation: The International Review of Science Fiction*. Her published short fiction includes lesbian romances "The Perfect Valentine" and "That Which Alters." Her recent short story, "A Mother's Milk," has been nominated for the 2018 Sunburst Award. Her three-year-old son always asks the best questions.

Amanda Roth teaches philosophy and women's and gender studies. She conducts academic research on the bioethics of **LGBTQ+** family-making and ethical issues related to pregnancy loss and abortion, drawing on her own experiences with these matters where possible. She lives in upstate New York with her wife, daughter and, living up to lesbian-cat-lady stereotypes as best she can, a gaggle of ex-feral, disabled and emotionally co-dependent cats.

Gail Marlene Schwartz's story, "Chosen," won third place in *Lilith Magazine*'s 2017 fiction contest. She's been anthologized in *Nature's Healing Spirit* (Sowing Creek Press, 2018), *Breaking Boundaries* (Rebel Mountain Press, 2017), *How to Expect What You're Not Expecting* (TouchWood Editions, 2013) and *Hidden Lives* (Brindle and Glass, 2017). Her work has also appeared or is forthcoming in the *New Quarterly*, *Room* magazine and *Poetica Magazine*. She is currently working on her first novel, in which "Loving Benjamin" is a chapter. gailmarleneschwartz.com.

Katie Taylor is a content writer and strategist. Her work has been featured in many online publications, including the *Washington Post* and the *Manifest Station*. She lives in the woods of Vermont with her wife, their son and an unruly dog.